Repurposing Legacy Data

Repurposing Legacy Data
Innovative Case Studies

Jules J. Berman

AMSTERDAM • BOSTON • HEIDELBERG • LONDON
NEW YORK • OXFORD • PARIS • SAN DIEGO
SAN FRANCISCO • SINGAPORE • SYDNEY • TOKYO

ELSEVIER

Elsevier
Radarweg 29, PO Box 211, 1000 AE Amsterdam, Netherlands
The Boulevard, Langford Lane, Kidlington, Oxford OX5 1GB, UK
225 Wyman Street, Waltham, MA 02451, USA

ISBN: 978-0-12-802882-7

British Library Cataloguing-in-Publication Data
A catalogue record for this book is available from the British Library

Library of Congress Cataloging-in-Publication Data
A catalog record for this book is available from the Library of Congress

For Information on all Elsevier publications,
visit our website at http://store.elsevier.com/

Working together
to grow libraries in
developing countries

www.elsevier.com • www.bookaid.org

CONTENTS

 **Jules J. Berman** holds two Bachelor of Science degrees from MIT (Mathematics, and Earth and Planetary Sciences), a PhD from Temple University, and an MD from the University of Miami. His postdoctoral studies were completed at the U.S. National Institutes of Health, and his medical residency was completed at the George Washington University Medical Center in Washington, DC. He served as Chief of Anatomic Pathology, Surgical Pathology, and Cytopathology at the Veterans Administration Medical Center in Baltimore, MD, where he held joint appointments at the University of Maryland Medical Center and at the Johns Hopkins Medical Institutions. In 1998, he became the Program Director for Pathology Informatics in the Cancer Diagnosis Program at the U.S. National Cancer Institute. In 2006, he was President of the Association for Pathology Informatics. In 2011, he received the Lifetime Achievement Award from the Association for Pathology Informatics. He has made many contributions to the field of data science, particularly in the areas of identification, deidentification, data exchange protocols, standards development, regulatory/legal issues, and metadata annotation. He is first author on over 100 journal articles and a coauthor on over 200 scientific publications. Today he is a freelance author, writing extensively in his three areas of expertise: informatics, computer programming, and medicine. A complete list of his publications is available at http://www.julesberman.info/pubs.htm.

CHAPTER 1

Introduction

1.1 WHY BOTHER?

We waste a lot of time waiting for spectacular new material.
We haven't sat down and taken a very close look at the material we have.
Bettina Stangneth, historian [1]

This book demonstrates how old data can be used in new ways that were not foreseen by the people who originally collected the data. All data scientists understand that there is much more old data than there is new data, and that the proportion of old data to new data will always be increasing (see Glossary item, New data). Two reasons account for this situation: (i) all new data becomes old data, with time and (ii) old data accumulates, without limit. If we are currently being flooded by new data, then we are surely being glaciated by old data.

Old data has enormous value, but we must be very smart if we hope to learn what the data is telling us. Data scientists interested in resurrecting old data must be prepared to run a gauntlet of obstacles. At the end of the gauntlet lies a set of unavoidable and important questions:

1. Can I actually use abandoned and ignored data to solve a problem that is worth solving?
2. Can old data be integrated into current information systems (databases, information systems, network resources) and made accessible, along with new data?
3. Will the availability of this old data support unknowable future efforts by other data scientists?
4. Can old data tell us anything useful about the world today and tomorrow?

A credible field of science cannot consist exclusively of promises for a bright future. As a field matures, it must develop its own written history, replete with successes and failures and a thoughtful answer to the question, "Was it worth the bother?" This book examines highlights in the history of data repurposing. In the process, you will encounter the general attitudes, skill sets, and approaches that have been the core, essential ingredients for successful repurposing projects. Specifically, this book provides answers to the following questions:

1. What are the kinds of data that are most suitable for data repurposing projects?
2. What are the fundamental chores of the data scientists who need to understand the content and potential value of old data?
3. How must data scientists prepare old data so that it can be understood and analyzed by future generations of data scientists?
4. How do innovators receive intellectual inspiration from old data?
5. What are the essential analytic techniques that are used in every data repurposing project?
6. What are the professional responsibilities of data scientists who use repurposed data?

The premise of this book is that data repurposing creates value where none was expected (see Glossary item, Data vs. datum). In some of the most successful data repurposing projects, analysts crossed scientific disciplines, to search for relationships that were unanticipated when the data was originally collected. We shall discover that the field of data repurposing attracts individuals with a wide range of interests and professional credentials. In the course of the book, we will encounter archeologists, astronomers, epigraphers, ontologists, cosmologists, entrepreneurs, anthropologists, forensic scientists, biomedical researchers, and many more (see Glossary item, Epigrapher). Anyone who needs to draw upon the general methods of data science will find this book useful. Although some of the case studies use advanced analytical techniques, most do not. It is surprising, but the majority of innovative data repurposing projects primarily involve simple counts of things. The innovation lies in the questions asked and the ability of the data repurposer to resurrect and organize information contained in old files. Accordingly, the book is written to be accessible to a diverse group of readers. Technical jargon is kept to a minimum, but unavoidable terminology is explained, at length, in an extensive Glossary.

1.2 WHAT IS DATA REPURPOSING?

If you want to make an apple pie from scratch, you must first create the universe.

Carl Sagan

Data repurposing involves taking preexisting data and performing any of the following:

1. Using the preexisting data to ask and answer questions that were not contemplated by the people who designed and collected the data (see Section 2.1)
2. Combining preexisting data with additional data, of the same kind, to produce aggregate data that suits a new set of questions that could not have been answered with any one of the component data sources (see Section 4.2)
3. Reanalyzing data to validate assertions, theories, or conclusions drawn from the original studies (see Section 5.1)
4. Reanalyzing the original data set using alternate or improved methods to attain outcomes of greater precision or reliability than the outcomes produced in the original analysis (see Section 5.3)
5. Integrating heterogeneous data sets (i.e., data sets with seemingly unrelated types of information), for the purpose of answering questions, or developing concepts, that span diverse scientific disciplines (see Section 4.3; Glossary item, Heterogeneous data)
6. Finding subsets in a population once thought to be homogeneous (see Section 5.4)
7. Seeking new relationships among data objects (see Section 3.1)
8. Creating, on-the-fly, novel data sets through data file linkages (see Section 2.5)
9. Creating new concepts or ways of thinking about old concepts, based on a re-examination of data (see Section 2.1)
10. Fine-tuning existing data models (see Section 4.2)
11. Starting over and remodeling systems (Section 2.3).

Most of the listed types of data repurposing efforts are self-explanatory and all of them will be followed by examples throughout this book. Sticklers may object to the inclusion of one of the items on the list, namely, "reanalyzing data to validate assertions, theories, or conclusions drawn from the original studies" (see Glossary item, Reanalysis). It can be argued that a reanalysis of data, for the purposes of validating a study, is an obligatory step in any well-designed project, done in conformance with the original purpose of the data; hence, reanalysis is not a form of data repurposing. If you believe that data reanalysis is a normal and usual process, you may wish to try a little experiment. Approach any scientist who has published his data analysis results in a journal. Indicate that you would like to reanalyze his results and conclusions, using your own preferred analytic techniques. Ask him to provide you with all of the data he used in his published study. Do not be surprised if your request is met with astonishment, horror, and a quick rebuff.

In general, scientists believe that their data is their personal property. Scientists may choose to share their data with bona fide collaborators, under their own terms, for a restricted purpose. In many cases, data sharing comes at a steep price (see Glossary item, Data sharing). A scientist who shares his data may stipulate that any future publications, based in whole or in part, on his data, must meet with his approval and must list him among the coauthors.

Because third-party reanalysis is seldom contemplated when scientists are preparing their data, I include it here as type of data repurposing (i.e., an unexpected way to use old data). Furthermore, data reanalysis often involves considerably more work than the original analysis, because data repurposers must closely analyze the manner in which the data was originally collected, must review the methods by which the data was prepared (i.e., imputing missing values, deleting outliers), and must develop various alternate methods of data analysis (see Glossary item, Missing values). A data reanalysis project, whose aim was to validate the original results, will often lead to new questions that were not entertained in the original study. Hence, data reanalysis and data repurposing are tightly linked concepts.

1.3 DATA WORTH PRESERVING

The first lesson of Web-scale learning is to use available large-scale data rather than hoping for annotated data that isn't available.
Peter Norvig, Alon Halevy, and Ferdinand Pereira [2]

Despite the preponderance of old data, most data scientists concentrate their efforts on newly acquired data or to nonexistent data that may emerge in the unknowable future. Why does old data get such little respect? The reasons are manifold.

1. Much of old data is proprietary and cannot be accessed by anyone other than its owners.
2. The owners of proprietary data, in many cases, are barely aware of the contents, or even the existence of their own data, and have no understanding of the value of their holdings, to themselves or to others.
3. Old data is typically stored in formats that are inscrutable to young data scientists. The technical expertise required to use the data intelligibly is long-forgotten.
4. Much of old data lacks proper annotation (see Glossary item, Annotation). There simply is not sufficient information about the data (e.g., how it was collected and what the data means) to support useful analysis.
5. Much of old data, annotated or not, has not been indexed in any serious way. There is no easy method of searching the contents of old data.
6. Much of old data is poor data, collected without the kinds of quality assurances that would be required to support any useful analysis of its contents.
7. Old data is orphaned data. When data has no guardianship, the tendency is to ignore the data or to greatly underestimate its value.

The sheer messiness of old data is conveyed by the gritty jargon that permeates the field of data repurposing (see Glossary items, Data cleaning, Data mining, Data munging, Data scraping, Data scrubbing, Data wrangling). Anything that requires munging, scraping, and scrubbing can't be too clean.

Data sources are referred to as "old" or "legacy"; neither term calls to mind vitality or robustness (see Glossary item, Legacy data). A helpful way of thinking about the subject is to recognize that new data is just updated old data. New data, without old data, cannot be used for the purpose of seeing long-term trends.

It may seem that nobody puts much value on legacy data; that nobody pays for legacy data, and that nobody invests in preserving legacy data. It is not surprising that nobody puts much effort into preserving data that has no societal value. The stalwart data scientist must not be discouraged. We shall see that preserving old data is worth the bother.

1.4 BASIC DATA REPURPOSING TOOLS

Another important early step is potentially time-consuming, but of great importance: sitting down with a large set of potential inputs and examining them by hand.... Four hours spent with a pile of articles and a highlighter may forestall many unpleasant surprises.

K. Bretonnel Cohen and Lawrence Hunter in an article entitled
"Getting Started in Text Mining" [3]

For any data repurposing project, these three freely available items will almost certainly come in handy.

1.4.1 A Simple Text Editor

When a large data file is encountered, the first step should involve reviewing the contents of the file. It is important to know whether the data is comprehensive (i.e., containing all of the data relevant to an intended purpose), representative (i.e., containing a useful number of data objects of every type of data included in the data set), reasonably organized (e.g., with identifiers for individual records and with a consistent set of features associated with each data record), and adequately annotated (e.g., timestamped appropriately and accompanied with descriptions of the data elements; see Glossary item, Time-stamp).

Perhaps the easiest way to review a large data file is to open it and browse, much the same way that you might browse the contents of books in a library. Most word processing software applications are not suited to opening and browsing large files, such as those exceeding about 50 MB in length. Text editors, unlike word processors, are designed to perform simple tasks on large, plain text files (i.e., unformatted text, also known as ASCII text), on the order of a gigabyte in length. There are many freely available text editors that can quickly open and search large files. Two popular and freely available text editors are Emacs and vi. Downloadable versions are available for Linux, Windows, and Macintosh systems. Text editors are useful for composing computer programs, which are always written in plain text. Data scientists will find it useful to acquire facility with a fast and simple text editor.

1.4.2 Simple Programming Skills

Like many individuals, I am not a cook. Nonetheless, I can prepare a few dishes when the need arises: scrambled eggs, oatmeal, and spaghetti. In a pinch, I'll open a can of tuna or baked beans. My wife insists that such activities do not qualify as cooking, but I maintain that the fundamental skills, such as heating, boiling, mixing, and measuring, are all there. It's cooking if I can eat it.

Programming for practitioners of data repurposing can be much like cooking for individuals who feel out-of-place in the kitchen. It would be a terrible mistake to surrender all programming chores to professional programmers. Each of us must have some programming skills, if we hope to survive as data professionals. Some of our most common and indispensable computational tasks are ridiculously easy to achieve, in any programming environment. We do not ask a master chef to fill a glass of water at the sink. Why would we seek the services of a professional programmer when we need to alphabetically sort a list or find records in a data set that match a query string, or annotate a collection of files with a name and date (see Glossary items, Query, String)? The bulk of the work involved in data repurposing projects will require skills in data organization, data curation, data annotation, data merging, data transforming, and a host of computationally simple techniques, that you should learn to do for yourself [4,5] (see Glossary items, Curation, Transformation).

There are hundreds of fine programming languages available; each with its own strengths and weaknesses. Perl, Python, and Ruby are powerful, no-cost programming languages, with versions available for most of the popular operating systems. Instructional online tutorials as well as a rich literature of print books provide nonprogrammers with the skills they will need, as data scientists [5–8]. If you intend to confine your programming efforts to simple tasks, such as basic arithmetic operations, simple descriptive statistics, search and replace methods, then you may wish to avoid the languages preferred by professional programmers use (e.g., C and Java). GUI (Graphic User Interface) languages such as Visual Basic require a level of programmatic overhead that you would probably not require. Specialty languages, such as R, for statistics, may come in handy, but they are not essential for every data scientist [9]. Some tasks should be left to specialists.

1.4.3 Data Visualization Utilities

For the eclectic scientist, Gnuplot or Matplotlib will cover all your data graphing needs. Gnuplot is an easy-to-use data visualization and analysis tool that is available at no cost [10]. Matplotlib is similar to Gnuplot, in terms of functionality, but it is designed to work within

Python scripts. Combined with a knowledge of Python, Matplotlib supports a remarkable range of data analysis options.

The outlook for data scientists who choose to be creative with their data has never been better. You can stop obsessing over your choice of operating system and programming language; modern scripting languages provide cross-platform compatibility. You can forget about buying expensive software applications; nearly everything you need is available at no cost. Feel free to think in terms of simple, no-cost utilities (e.g., command-line programs or specialized modules) that will implement specific algorithms, as required (see Glossary item, Algorithm). Write your own short scripts designed to perform one particular computational task, quickly, using a minimal amount of code and without the overhead of a graphic user interface. A few hours of effort will start you on your way towards data independence.

1.5 PERSONAL ATTRIBUTES OF DATA REPURPOSERS

What is needed is not only people with a good background in a particular field, but also people capable of making a connection between item 1 and item 2 which might not ordinarily seem connected.

Isaac Asimov [11]

By far, the most important asset of any data analyst is her brain. A set of personal attributes that include critical thinking, an inquisitive mind, the patience to spend hundreds of hours reviewing data, is certain to come in handy.

Expertise in analytic algorithms is an overrated skill. Most data analysis projects require the ability to understand the data, and this can often be accomplished with simple data visualization tools. The application of rigorous mathematical and statistical algorithms typically comes at the end of the project, after the key relationships among data objects are discovered (see Glossary item, Data object). It is important to remember that if your old data is verified, organized, annotated, and preserved, the analytic process can be repeated and improved. In most cases, the first choice of analytic method is not the best choice. No single analytic method is critical when the data analyst has the opportunity to repeat his work applying many different methods, all the while attaining a better understanding of the data and more meaningful computational results.

1.5.1 Data Organization Methods

Everyone who enters the field of data science dreams of using advanced analytic techniques to solve otherwise intractable problems. In reality, much of data science involves collecting, cleaning, organizing, annotating, transforming, and integrating data. For reasons that will become apparent in later chapters, repurposing projects will require more data organization than "fresh data" projects. There are established techniques whereby data is usefully organized, and these techniques should be learned and practiced. Individuals who are willing to spend a considerable portion of their time organizing data will be in the best position to benefit from data repurposing projects.

1.5.2 Ability to Develop a Clear Understanding of the Goals of a Project

It is often remarked that members of an interdisciplinary team find it difficult to communicate with one another. They all seem to be babbling in different languages. How can a biologist understand the thoughts and concerns of a statistician; or vice versa? In many cases, communication barriers that arise in multidisciplinary repurposing projects result from the narrow focus of individual team members; not in their inability to communicate. If everyone on a data repurposing team is pursuing a different set of project goals, it is unlikely that they will be able to communicate effectively with one another.

It is crucial that everyone involved in a data repurposing project must come to the same, clear understanding of the project. Failure comes when team members lose track of the overall goal of a project and lack any realistic sense of the steps involved in reaching the goal [12]. When every project member understands the contributions of every other project member, most of the communication problems disappear.

In future chapters, we shall see that the most important and most innovative repurposing projects involve multiple individuals, from diverse disciplines, who use the achievements of their co-workers to advance toward a common goal.

REFERENCES

[1] Schuessler J. Book portrays Eichmann as evil, but not banal. The New York Times September 2, 2014.

[2] Norvig P, Halevy A, Pereira F. The unreasonable effectiveness of data. IEEE Intell Syst 2009;24:8−12.

[3] Cohen KB, Hunter L. Getting started in text mining. PLoS Comput Biol 2008;4:e20.

[4] Berman JJ. Principles of big data: preparing, sharing, and analyzing complex information. Burlington, MA: Morgan Kaufmann; 2013.

[5] Berman JJ. Biomedical informatics. Sudbury, MA: Jones and Bartlett; 2007.

[6] Berman JJ. Perl programming for medicine and biology. Sudbury, MA: Jones and Bartlett; 2007.

[7] Berman JJ. Methods in medical informatics: fundamentals of healthcare programming in perl, python, and ruby. Boca Raton, FL: Chapman and Hall; 2010.

[8] Berman JJ. Ruby programming for medicine and biology. Sudbury, MA: Jones and Bartlett; 2008.

[9] Lewis PD. R for medicine and biology. Sudbury, MA: Jones and Bartlett Publishers; 2009.

[10] Janert PK. Gnuplot in action: understanding data with graphs. Shelter Island, NY: Manning; 2009.

[11] Asimov I. Isaac asimov mulls "How do people get new ideas?" MIT Technol Rev 2014.

[12] Basili VR, Perricone BT. Software errors and complexity: an empirical investigation. Commun ACM 1984;27:556−63.

CHAPTER 2

Learning from the Masters

2.1 NEW PHYSICS FROM OLD DATA

All science is description and not explanation.
Karl Pearson, The Grammar of Science, Preface to 2nd edition, 1899

Case Study 2.1: Sky Charts

For most of us, the positions of the planets and of the stars do not provide us with any useful information. This was not always so. For a large part of the history of mankind, individuals determined their locations, the date, and the time, from careful observations of the night sky. On a cloudless night, a competent navigator, on the sea or in the air, could plot a true course.

Repurposed data from old star charts was used to settle and unsettle one of our greatest mysteries; earth's place in the universe. Seven key scientists, working in tandem over a period of four centuries, used night sky data to reach profound and shocking conclusions: Aristarchus of Samos (circa 310–230 BCE), Nicolaus Copernicus (1473–1543), Tycho Brahe (1546–1601), Johannes Kepler (1571–1630), Galileo Galilei (1564–1642), Isaac Newton (1643–1727), and Albert Einstein (1879–1955).

Back in the third century BCE, Aristarchus of Samos studied the night sky and reasoned that the earth and planets orbited the sun. In addition, Aristarchus correctly assigned the relative positions of the known planets to their heliocentric orbits. About 1,800 years later, Copernicus reanalyzed Aristachus' assertions to confirm the heliocentric orbits of the planets, and plotted their elliptic trajectories. Soon thereafter, Tycho Brahe produced improved star charts, bequeathing this data to his student, Johannes Kepler. Kepler used the charts to derive three general laws describing the movement of planets. In 1687, Newton published his Principia, wherein Kepler's empiric laws, based on observational data, were redeveloped from physical principles, Newton's laws of motion. Newton's contribution was a remarkable example of data modeling, wherein an equation was created to describe a set of data pertaining to physical objects (see Glossary item, Modeling).

As is almost always the case, this multigenerational repurposing project led to a conceptual simplification of the original data. After the switch was made from a geocentric to a heliocentric system, operating under a simple set of equations, it became far easier to calculate the relative motion of objects (e.g., planetary orbits) and to predict the position of celestial bodies.

From Newton's work, based on Kepler's elliptical orbits, based in turn on Tycho Brahe's data, came the calculus and Newton's theory of relativity. Newton, as well as his predecessor Galileo, assumed the existence of an absolute space, within which the laws of motion hold true. The planets, and all physical bodies, were thought to move relative to one another in their own frames of reference, within an absolute space, all sharing an absolute time. Einstein revisited Newton's theories of relativity and concluded that time, like motion, is relative and not absolute.

The discovery of heliocentric planetary motion and the broader issues of relative frames of observation in space were developed over more than 2,000 years of observation, analysis, and reanalysis of old data. Each successive scientist used a prior set of observations to answer a new question. In so doing, star data, originally intended for navigational purposes, was repurposed to produce a new model of our universe.

Case Study 2.2: From Hydrogen Spectrum Data to Quantum Mechanics

In about 1880, Vogel and Huggins published the emission frequencies of hydrogen (i.e., the hydrogen spectroscopic emission lines) [1,2]. In 1885, Johann Balmer, studying the emission frequencies of the hydrogen spectral lines, developed a formula that precisely expressed frequency in terms of the numeric order of its emission line (i.e., $n = 1, 2, 3, 4$, and so on). Balmer's attempt at data modeling produced one of the strangest equations in the history of science. There was simply no precedent for expressing the frequency of an electromagnetic wave in terms of its spectral emission rank. The formula was introduced to the world without the benefit of any theoretical explanation. Balmer himself indicated that he was just playing around with numbers. Nonetheless, he had hit upon a formula that precisely described multiple emission lines, in terms of ascending integers.

Twenty-eight years later, Niels Bohr, in 1913, chanced upon Balmer's formula and used it to explain spectral lines in terms of energy emissions resulting from transitions between discrete electron orbits. Balmer's amateurish venture into data repurposing led, somewhat inadvertently, to the birth of modern quantum physics.

2.2 REPURPOSING THE PHYSICAL AND ABSTRACT PROPERTY OF UNIQUENESS

L'art c'est moi, la science c'est nous.

Claude Bernard

An object is unique if it can be distinguished from every other object. The quality of object uniqueness permits data scientists to associate non-unique data values with unique data objects; hence, identifying the data. As an example, let us examine the utility of natural uniqueness for the forensic scientist.

Case Study 2.3: Fingerprints; from Personal Identifier to Data-Driven Forensics

Fingerprints have been used, since antiquity, as a method for establishing the identity of individuals. Fingerprints were pressed onto clay tablets, seals, and even pottery left by ancient civilizations that included Minoan, Greek, Japanese, and Chinese. As early as the second millennium BCE, fingerprints were used as a type of signature in Babylon, and ancient Babylonian policemen recorded the fingerprints of criminals, much as modern policemen do today (Figure 2.1).

Figure 2.1 U.S. Federal Bureau of Investigation Fingerprint Division, World War II. FBI, public domain (see Glossary item, Public domain).

Towards the close of the nineteenth century, Francis Galton repurposed fingerprint data to pursue his own particular interests. Galton was primarily interested in the heritability and racial characteristics of fingerprints, a field of study that can best be described as a scientific dead end. Nonetheless, in pursuit of his interests, he devised a way of classifying fingerprints by patterns (e.g., plain arch, tented arch, simple loop, central pocket loop, double loop, lateral pocket loop, and plain whorl). This classification launched the new science of fingerprint identification, an area of research that has been actively pursued and improved over the past 120 years (see Glossary item, Classification).

In addition to Galton's use of classification methods, two closely related simple technological enhancements vastly increased the importance of fingerprints. The first was the incredibly simple procedure of recording sets of fingerprints, on paper, with indelible ink. With the simple fingerprint card, the quality of fingerprints improved, and the process of sharing and comparing recorded fingerprints became more practical. The second enhancement was the decision to collect fingerprint cards in permanent population databases. Fingerprint databases enabled forensic scientists to match fingerprints found at the scene of a crime, with fingerprints stored in the database. The task of fingerprint matching was greatly simplified by confining comparisons to prints that shared the same class-based profiles, as described by Galton.

Repurposing efforts have expanded the use of fingerprints to include authentication (i.e., proving you are who you claim to be), keying (e.g., opening locked devices based on an authenticated fingerprint or some other identifying biometric), tracking (e.g., establishing the path and whereabouts of an individual by following a trail of fingerprints or other identifiers), and body part identification (i.e., identifying the remains of individuals recovered from mass graves or from the sites of catastrophic events). In the past decade, flaws in the vaunted process of fingerprint identification have been documented, and the improvement of the science of identification is an active area of investigation [3].

Today, most of what we think of as the forensic sciences is based on object identification (e.g., biometrics, pollen identification, trace chemical investigation, tire mark investigation, and so on). When a data object is uniquely identified, its association with additional data can be collected, aggregated, and retrieved, as needed.

2.3 REPURPOSING A 2,000-YEAR-OLD CLASSIFICATION

Our similarities are different.

Yogi Berra

Classifications drive down the complexity of knowledge domains and lay bare the relationships among different objects. Observations that hold for a data object may also hold for the other objects of the same class and for their class descendants (see Glossary item, Class). The data analyst can develop and test hypotheses by collecting representative objects belonging to different classes and determining whether the other members of the class exhibit the same features. For example, a researcher may hypothesize that an antibiotic that kills a particular infectious organism may be equally effective against all of the various species that belong to the same biological class. A dataset that assigns a class to each organism would permit the researcher to test the hypothesis.

Case Study 2.4: A Dolphin Is Not a Fish

Nothing in biology makes sense except in the light of evolution
Theodosius Dobzhansky, evolutionary biologist, in a 1973 essay

Aristotle (384–322 BCE) was one of the first philosophers to think deeply about classifications, and how they can be used to determine the order and nature of the natural world. He and his followers undertook the classification of all living organisms, a project that has continued up to the present day. For modern biologists, the key to the classification of living organisms is evolutionary descent (i.e., phylogeny). The hierarchy of classes corresponds to the succession of organisms evolving from the earliest living organism to the current set of extant species.

The 1909 discovery of the Burgess shale, by Charles Walcott, revealed the chronologic evolution of life forms through ascending rock strata. The Burgess shale provided taxonomists with an opportunity to determine the epoch in which classes of organisms first came into existence and the relative order of precedence of the identified fossil species. Late in the twentieth century, taxonomists could study the sequences of nucleic acids in the genes of various organisms. This data revealed the divergence of shared genes among related organisms and added greatly to our understanding of every class of organism living on earth today.

Pre-Darwinian biologists, who knew nothing about evolution, who had no access to the Burgess shale, and for whom genetic sequences had no meaning whatsoever, had somehow produced a classification of organisms that looks remarkably similar to the classification we use today (Figure 2.2).

How did the early taxonomists arrive so close to our modern taxonomy, without the benefit of the principles of evolution, modern paleontological discoveries, or molecular biology (see Glossary item, Taxonomy)? For example, how was it possible for Aristotle to know,

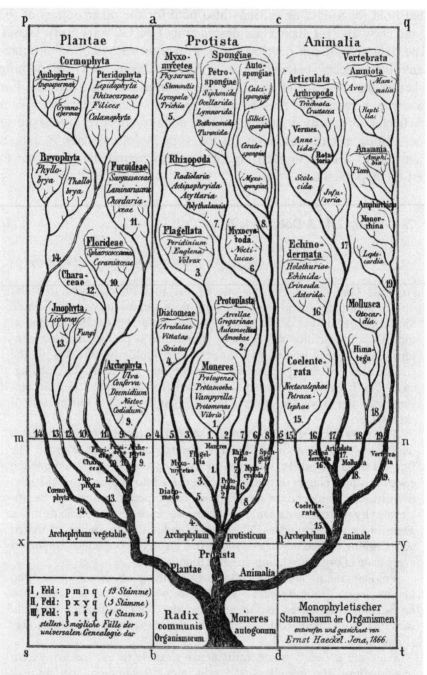

Figure 2.2 Ernst Haeckel's rendition of the classification of living organisms, circa 1866. Wikipedia, public domain.

2,000 years ago, that a dolphin is a mammal and not a fish? Aristotle studied the anatomy and the developmental biology of many different types of animals. One class of animals was distinguished by a gestational period in which a developing embryo is nourished by a placenta, and the offspring is delivered into the world as formed, but small versions of the adult animals (i.e., not as eggs or larvae), and in which the newborn animals feed from milk excreted from nipples, overlying specialized glandular organs in the mother (mammae). Aristotle knew that these were features that specifically characterized one group of animals and distinguished this group from all the other groups of animals. He also knew that dolphins had all these features; fish did not. From these observations, he correctly reasoned that dolphins were a type of mammal, not a type of fish. Aristotle was ridiculed by his contemporaries for whom it was obvious that a dolphin is a fish. Unlike Aristotle, they based their classification on similarities, not on relationships. They saw that dolphins looked like fish and dolphins swam in the ocean like fish, and this was all the proof they needed.

For nearly 2,000 years following the death of Aristotle, biologists persisted in their belief that dolphins were a type of fish. Not until the past several hundred years have biologists acknowledged that Aristotle was correct; dolphins are mammals. Aristotle had demonstrated that shared properties characterize classes of animals, accounting for the uniqueness of each class of organism. In later chapters, we will see that the same principles developed by Aristotle to classify dolphins as mammals can be used to classify data objects within a knowledge domain.

Case Study 2.5: The Molecular Stopwatch

The cell is basically an historical document.

Carl Woese [4]

Carl Woese (1928–2012) was one of the most influential contributors to the field of molecular phylogenetics. By observing changes in the sequences of ribosomal RNA, Woese and his colleagues determined the branchings, over time, that occur during the evolution of organisms.

Ribosomal RNA has been one of the most intensively studied molecules in molecular biology, because these molecules coordinate the translation of messenger RNA into protein. Every living creature on earth synthesizes ribosomal RNA. Hence, it is inferred that every molecule of ribosomal RNA on earth today evolved from a genetic sequence coding for ribosomal RNA that was present in one of the first life forms to appear on this planet. The gene sequences coding for ribosomal RNA have been studied for the purpose of understanding the morphology, functionality, and control mechanisms that apply to this ubiquitous molecule. Carl Woese studied sequence data for ribosomal RNA in a range of organisms, but he did so for a purpose totally unrelated to any of the questions being pursued by his contemporaries.

Woese reasoned that if ribosomal RNA is present in every organism on earth, and if it performs roughly the same function in every organism on earth, and if that function is vital to every cell in every organism on earth, then the gene sequence coding for ribosomal RNA must change very slowly over aeons of time, and that these slow changes in the sequence of RNA can be followed through the evolutionary lineage of organisms. Using the sequence of ribosomal RNA as an evolutionary stopwatch, Woese reconstructed the phylogeny of life on this planet, starting with the first living organisms [4,5].

Prior to the work of Woese and others, in the 1990s, there was little hope that simple bacteria could be classified sensibly into a phylogenetic hierarchy. During the several billion years of bacterial evolution, it was likely that primitive organisms merged with one another. There is every reason to believe that early viruses pulled and pushed fragments of DNA among many different bacterial organisms. It is even possible that native molecules of DNA, formed in the primordial soup of ancient earth, were acquired by members of different branches of evolving organisms. Biologists expected that these promiscuous exchanges of genetic material would have created a collection of different bacterial organisms for which a strict phylogenetic classification (i.e., a classification by ancestral descent) was impossible to construct. It came as a great surprise to many when Woese and others developed a robust phylogenetic classification of bacteria based on their analyses of a single molecule, ribosomal RNA. Out of his early work, came a newly recognized kingdom of life, the Archaean prokaryotes, which were shown to have variations in their ribosomal RNA sequence, that are not found in bacteria or in bacterial descendants and which could not have evolved from bacteria. Today, the class of Archaean organisms stands alongside the bacteria as one of the earliest and most enduring organisms on the planet.

As with much of science, Woese's theories attract controversy [6—8]. The point made here is that repurposing ribosomal sequence data, from the realm of molecular biology to the realm of biological evolution, revitalized the staid field of evolutionary biology.

2.4 DECODING THE PAST

It is an amazement, how the voice of a person long dead can speak to you off a page as a living presence.

Garrison Keillor

Case Study 2.6: Mayan Glyphs: Finding a Lost Civilization

On the Yucatan peninsula, concentrated within a geographic area that today encompasses the southeastern tip of Mexico, plus Belize, and Guatemala, a great civilization flourished. The Mayan civilization seems to have begun about 2000 BCE, reaching its peak in the so-called classic period (250–900 AD). Abruptly, about 900 AD, the great Mayan cities were abandoned, and the Mayan civilization entered a period of decline. Soon after the Spanish colonization of the peninsula, in the sixteenth century, the Mayans were subjected to a deliberate effort to erase any trace of their heritage. The desecration of the Mayans was led by a Spanish priest named Diego de Landa Calderon (1524–1579). Landa's acts against Mayan culture included:

1. The destruction of all Mayan books and literature (only a few books survived immolation).
2. The conversion of Mayans to Catholicism, in which school children were forced to learn Roman script and Arabic numerals.
3. The importation of the Spanish Inquisition, accounting for the deaths of many Mayans who preferred their own culture over that of Landa's.

By the dawn of the twentieth century, the great achievements of the Mayan civilization were forgotten, its cities and temples were overgrown by jungle, its books had been destroyed, and no humans on the planet could decipher the enduring stone glyph tablets strewn through the Yucatan peninsula (Figure 2.3).

Figure 2.3 Mayan glyphs, displayed in Palenque Museum, Chiapas, Mexico. Wikipedia, public domain.

In the late twentieth century, culminating several centuries of effort by generations of archeologists and epigraphers, the Maya glyphs were successfully decoded. The successful decoding of the Mayan glyphs and the discovery of the history and achievements of the Mayan civilization, during its classic period, is, perhaps, the most exciting legacy data project ever undertaken. The story of the resurrection and translation of the Mayan glyphs leaves us with many lessons that apply to modern-day data repurposing projects.

Lesson 1: Success Follows Multiple Breakthroughs, Sometimes Occurring Over Great Lengths of Time

The timetable for the Mayan glyph project extends over more than three centuries.

1566—Landa, the same man largely responsible for the destruction of the Mayan culture and language, wrote a manuscript in which he attempted to record a one-to-one correspondence between the Roman alphabet and the Mayan alphabet, with the help of local Mayans. Landa had assumed that the Mayan language was alphabetic, like the Spanish language. As it happens, the Mayan language is logophonetic, with some symbols corresponding to syllables and other symbols corresponding to words and concepts. For centuries, the so-called Mayan alphabet only added to the general confusion. Eventually, Landa's notes were repurposed, along with the few surviving Mayan codices, to crack the Mayan code.

1832—Constantine Rafinesque decoded the Mayan number system.

1880—Forstemann, working from an office in Dresden, Germany, had access to the Dresden Codex, one of the few surviving Mayan manuscripts. Using Rafinesque's techniques to decode the numbers that appeared in the Dresden Codex, Forstemann deduced how the Mayans recorded the passage of time, and how they used numbers to predict astronomic events.

1952—Yuri Knorosov, working alone in Russia, deduced how individual glyph symbols were used as syllables.

1958—Tatiana Proskouriakoff, using Knorosov's syllabic approach to glyph interpretation, convincingly made the first short translations from stelae (i.e., standing stone monuments), and proved that they told the life stories of Mayan kings.

1973—30 Mayanists from various scientific disciplines convened at a Palenque, a Mayan site, and, through a team effort, deciphered the dynastic history of six kings.

1981—David Stuart showed that different pictorial symbols could represent the same symbol, so long as the beginning sound of the word represented by the symbol was the same as the beginning sound of the other syllable-equivalent words. This would be analogous to a picture of a ball, a balance, and a banner, all serving as interchangeable forms of the sound "ba."

Following Stuart's 1981 breakthrough, the Mayan code was essentially broken.

Lesson 2: Contributions Come from Individuals Working in Isolation and Individuals Working as a Team

My feeling is that as far as creativity is concerned, isolation is required.
Isaac Asimov [9]

As social animals, we tend to believe in the supremacy of teamwork. We often marginalize the contributions of individuals who work in isolation. Objective review of most large, successful projects reveals that important contributions come from individuals working in isolation, plus teams, working to accomplish goals that could not be achieved through the efforts of an individual. The task of decoding the Mayan glyphs was assisted by two key individuals, each working in isolation, thousands of miles from Mexico: Ernst Forstemann, in Germany, and Yuri Knorozov, in Moscow. It is difficult to imagine how the Mayan project could have succeeded without the contributions of these two loners. The remainder of the project was accomplished within a community of scientists who cleared the long forgotten Mayan cities, recovered glyphs, compared the findings at the different sites, and eventually reconstructed the language. Throughout this book, we will examine legacy projects that succeeded due to the combined efforts of teams and of isolated individuals.

Lesson 3: Project Contributors Come from Many Different Disciplines

The team of 30 experts convening in Palenque, in 1973 was composed of archeologists, epigraphers, linguists, anthropologists, historians, astronomers, and ecologists.

Lesson 4: Progress Was Delayed Due to Influential Naysayers

After the Mayan numbering system had been decoded, and after it was shown that the Mayans were careful recorders of time, and astronomic events, linguists turned their attention to the fascinating legacy of the nonnumeric glyphs. Try as they might, Mayanists of the mid-twentieth century could make no sense of the nonnumeric symbols. Eric Thompson (1898–1975) stood as the premier Mayanist authority from the 1930s through the 1960s. After trying, and failing, to decipher the nonnumeric glyphs, he concluded that these glyphs represented mystic, ornate symbols; not language. The nonnumeric glyphs, in his opinion, could not be deciphered because they had no linguistic meaning. Thompson was venerated to such an extent that, throughout his long tenure of influence, all progress in the area of glyph translation was suspended. Not until Thompson's influence finally waned, could a new group of Mayanists come forward to crack the code.

Lesson 5: Ancient Legacy Data Conformed to Modern Annotation Practices

The original data had a set of properties that were conducive to repurposing: unique, identified objects (e.g., name of king and name of city, with a timestamp on all entries, implying the existence of a sophisticated calendar and time-keeping methods). The data was encoded in a sophisticated number system, that included the concept of zero, and was annotated with metadata (i.e., descriptions of the quantitative data; see Glossary item, Metadata).

Lesson 6: Legacy Data Is Often Highly Accurate Data

Old data is often accurate data, if it is recorded at the time and place that events transpired. Records of crops, numbers of sacrifices, numbers of slaves traded, are examples. In the astronomical data included in the Dresden Codex, Mayan astronomers accurately predicted eclipses, measuring decade-long intervals, accurate to within several minutes.

Lesson 7: Legacy Data Is Necessary for Following Trends

There is a tendency to be dismissive of archeologic data due to the superabundance of more recently acquired data (see Glossary item, Data archeology). A practical way to think about the value of archeological data is that if the total amount of historical data is relatively small, the absolute value of each piece of such data is high. For example, year 1990 records on temperature and precipitation may not exhibit the level of detail contained in present-day meteorological files, but the 1990 files may represent the only reliable source of climate data for the era. Without the availability of old data, that establishes baseline measurements and trends, the analysis of new data is impeded. Hence, every bit of old data has amplified importance for today's data scientists. The classic empire of the Mayans came to an abrupt ending, about 900 AD. We do not understand the reason for the collapse of Mayan civilization, but untapped clues residing in the Mayan glyphs may reveal disturbing ancient trends that presage a future catastrophe.

Lesson 8: Data Worth Recording Is Data Worth Saving

Landa destroyed the Mayan libraries in 1562. The few remaining literary works of the ancient Mayans can be translated, but the vast bulk of Mayan literature is a lost legacy. Any one of those formerly disparaged books would be a priceless treasure today.

Book burnings are a time-honored tradition enjoyed the world over by religious zealots [10]. Some of the greatest books in history have been burned to a crisp. The first recorded, but least successful, book burning in history occurred around 612 BC and involved the library of Ashurbanipal (668–627 BC), king of the neo-Assyrian empire. Among the texts contained in the library was the Gilgamesh epic, written in about 2,500 BC Marauders set fire to the palace and the library, with limited effect. Many of the texts were written on cuneiform tablets. The fire baked the clay tablets, preserving them to the present day. The Library of Alexandria was the most famous library of the ancient world. As a repository of truth and knowledge, it was a popular target for book burners. At least four major assaults punctuated the library's incendiary past: Julius Caesar in the Alexandrian War (48 BC), Aurelian's Palmyrine campaign (273 AD), the decree of Theophilus (391 AD), and the Muslim conquest (642 AD). We do not know the number of books held in the Library, but when the Alexandria library was sacked, the books provided sufficient fuel to heat the Roman baths for 6 months. Book burning never goes out of style. As recently as 1993, during the siege of Sarajevo, the National Library was enthusiastically burned to the ground. Thousands of irreplaceable books were destroyed in the literary equivalent of genocide.

2.5 WHAT MAKES DATA USEFUL FOR REPURPOSING PROJECTS?

Every increased possession loads us with new weariness.
John Ruskin, author, art critic, and social reformer (1819–1900)

Is there any way of setting a value on legacy data? Can we predict which datasets will be most useful for data repurposing projects? Of course, the value of data is, like everything else, relative. A library of Mayan glyphs may be of relatively little value to a particle physicist, but of relatively great value to the curator of a Mesoamerican art collection (see Glossary item, Curator). Still, based on our observations of several successful data repurposing projects, we can generalize that any one of the following five qualities will greatly enhance the value of legacy data.

1. Data that establishes uniqueness or identity
2. Data that accrues over time, documenting the moments when data objects are obtained (i.e., timestamped data)
3. Data that establishes membership in a defined group or class
4. Data that is classified for every object in a knowledge domain
5. Introspective data—data that explains itself.

Let us take a moment to examine each of these data features.

Data That Establishes Uniqueness or Identity

The most useful repurposed data establishes the identity of objects. This generalization has applied to all of our previous examples of data repurposing, reviewed in this chapter. We shall see, in Section 6.5, that we can provide data objects with unique identifiers. In many cases, objects have their own, natural identifiers that come very close to establishing uniqueness. Examples include fingerprints, iris patterns, and the sequence of nucleotides in an organism's genetic material.

Case Study 2.7: CODIS

With the exception of identical twins, parthenogenetic offspring, and clones, every organism on earth has a unique sequence of DNA-forming nucleotides that distinguishes its genetic material (i.e., it's genome) from the genome of every other organism (see Glossary item, Parthenogenesis). If we were to have a record of the complete sequence of nucleotides in an individual's genome, we could distinguish that individual from every other organism on earth, by comparing genome sequences. This would be a difficult undertaking, as the human genome is 3 billion nucleotides in length. Because there is enormous variability in the genetic sequences of individuals, the identity of human individuals can be established by sampling just 13 short segments of DNA.

CODIS (Combined DNA Index System) collects the unique nucleotide sequences of the equivalent 13 segments of DNA, for every individual included in the database [11]. Using CODIS, DNA sampled at a crime scene can be matched against DNA samples contained in the database. Hence, the identity of individuals whose DNA is found at a crime scene can often be established. In the absence of a match, it is sometimes possible to establish the genetic relationship (i.e., paternal or maternal relatives) between crime scene samples and individuals included in the database.

CODIS serves an example of database with narrow scope (i.e., names of people and associated DNA sequences), and broad societal value. The basic design of the CODIS database can be extended to any organism. For example, a database of DNA samples collected from individual trees in a geographic location can establish the source of seeds or pollen grains sticking to an article of clothing, and this information might lead to the location where a criminal event transpired. A population database containing full genome DNA sequences could be used to determine the presence or absence of disease-causing genes in individuals or to predict the response of an individual to a particular drug [12–15].

Data That Accrues Over Time, Documenting the Moments When Data Objects Are Obtained (i.e., Timestamped Data)

We need above all to know about changes; no one wants or needs to be reminded 16 hours a day that his shoes are on.

David Hubel

When a dataset contains data records that collect over time, it becomes possible to measure how the attributes of data records may change as the data accumulates. Signal analysts use the term "time series" to refer to attribute measurements that change over time. The shape of the time series can be periodic (i.e., repeating over specific intervals), linear, nonlinear, Gaussian, or multimodal (i.e., having multiple peaks and troughs). A large part of data science is devoted to finding trends in data, determining simple functions that model the variation of data over time, or predicting how data will change in the future. All these analytic activities require data that is annotated with the time that a measurement is made, or the time that a record is prepared, or the time that an event has occurred.

You may be shocked to learn that many, if not most, web pages lack a timestamp to signify the date and time when the page's textual content was created. This oversight applies to news reports, announcements from organizations and governments, and even scientific papers; all being instances for which a timestamp would seem to be an absolute necessity. When a scientist publishes an undated manuscript, how would anyone know if the results are novel? If a news article describes an undated event, how would anyone know whether the report is current? For the purposes of data analysis, undated documents and data records are useless.

Whereas undated documents have very little value, all transactions, statements, documents, and data points that are annotated with reliable timestamps will always have some value, particularly if the information continues to collect over time. This statement holds true even when the data seems to be of a trivial nature at the time it was collected. For example, if a curious astronomer was to take a photo of the sun at the same time, place, and camera angle, every day, for a year, and if each photograph were marked with the date, and time, she might stand to learn a great deal about the orbit of the earth around the sun, the seasons, the location of the camera on the planet, weather patterns associated with dates, the types of birds that inhabit the sky at different times of the year, the condition of vegetation through the year, and much more. If the photographs are undated, then the potential benefit of the photographs is lost.

Many of the scribes and data curators from ancient civilizations understood the importance of timestamping. It is common to find dates engraved on obelisks, steles, monuments, and other permanent data markers. For the Mayans, dates were important for their association with the reign of a particular king, season, and astronomical position. Because ancient Mayan script, as a rule, comes with a date, modern archeologists can reconstruct a progression of events marking the rise and fall of the Colombian period.

Today, anyone with a computer can easily timestamp their data, with the date and the time, accurate to within a second (see Glossary item, Accuracy vs. precision). I happen to be composing this paragraph using a text editor that inserts a timestamp into the text whenever and wherever I push the "F5" key, just so: "(date 2014/10/23, time 11:51, seconds 37)". The programmer who wrote the editing software must have understood the value of documenting time, and that is why he designed a timestamp function that executes at the push of a single key.

Time data can be formatted in any of dozens of ways, all of which can be instantly converted to an international standard (i.e., the ISO 8601 date and time standard) [16] (see Glossary item, ISO). For a host of inadequate reasons, the consistent application of a simple timestamp to documents and data is a neglected habit. A good deal of society's legacy data cannot be repurposed, simply because we do not know the time that it was collected.

Data That Establishes Membership in a Defined Group or Class

If we know that a data object belongs to a well-defined group of objects, we can evaluate the features of the group and infer properties of group members that lack measured data. For example, if we know that an individual drives a Porsche, and we know that the average income of Porsche owners is $200,000 per year, then we can reasonably guess that the individual has a large income. Data establishing class membership is particularly useful in the field of predictive analytics.

Case Study 2.8: Zip Codes: From Postal Code to Demographic Keystone

There are three ways to assign integers to objects: cardinals, ordinal, and nominals. Cardinals tell us the number of objects (e.g., 2, 5, or 10 items). Ordinals give us a rank (e.g., 1st, or 5th, or 8th place in a list). Nominal means "in name only," and nominals are arbitrary numbers that help identify an object. Telephone numbers, social security numbers, and zip codes are nominals. Nominals can be added together or multiplied, and divided, but it would be pointless to do so. Despite its self-effacing definition and its limited mathematical utility, nominal datasets are among the most useful of legacy data resources.

Zip codes were contrived by the U.S. Postal service to speed the distribution of mail. The original 5-digit zip codes were introduced in the early 1960s, with each zip code representing a geographic area containing a roughly equivalent segment of the population. The first three digits of the zip code identify mail distribution centers, from which mail sorted by the remaining two digits is distributed to the proper post offices. In the 1980s, an additional 4 digits was appended to the zip code, identifying individual buildings within the boundary of the 5-digit code.

Because zip codes describe geographic and demographic areas, they can be assigned a longitude, latitude, and elevation, typically measured at the geographic center of its boundaries. All data to which a zip code is attached (e.g., addresses, charge card transactions, crime reports, occurrences of reportable diseases, deaths, electricity consumption, water resources, homes receiving cable television, broadband usage) can be organized with the zip code serving as its primary record key. The lowly zip code, intended as an aid to mail men, has been repurposed to serve entrepreneurs, epidemiologists, resource managers, and many others.

Data That Is Classified for Every Object in a Knowledge Domain

The premise that will be repeated throughout this book is that data analysis is primarily concerned with finding relationships among data objects. For example, is a certain object different from another object, or is it a subtype of the object? If it is different from the other object, how does its value change when the value of other object changes?

The relationships among the different objects in a knowledge domain can be encapsulated by a classification (see Glossary item, Encapsulation). A classification, as used herein, is a hierarchy of objects that conforms to the following principles:

1. The classes (i.e., groups containing members) of the hierarchy have a set of properties or rules that extend to every member of the class and to all of the subclasses of the class. A subclass is itself a type of class wherein the members retain properties of the parent class and have some additional property or properties specific for the subclass.
2. In a hierarchical classification, each subclass may have no more than one direct superclass (i.e., the parent class). The root (top) class has no parent class (see Glossary items, Child class, Parent class, Subclass, Superclass). The biological classification of living organisms is a hierarchical classification. In the case of the classification of living organisms, the bottom class of the hierarchy is known as the species and contains the individuals belonging to the species (e.g., every squirrel belongs to a species of "squirrel").
3. Classes and species are intransitive. A member of a class does not leave its class to become a member of another class (e.g., a horse never becomes a sheep).

4. The members of classes may be highly similar to each other, but their similarities result from their membership in the same class and not the other way around (see Glossary item, Similarity vs. Relationship).
5. A robust classification is complete (i.e., a place for every object, and every object in its place). Pseudoclasses, such as "miscellaneous objects" or "unclassified objects," indicate that the classification lacks robustness.

If the data analyst begins her investigations with an established classification, and if each of the data objects included in the legacy data set has been assigned a class within the classification, then the task of testing hypotheses becomes much easier.

It must be noted that the term "classification," as used herein, is not closely related to the term "classifier," as commonly used by data scientists. Classifiers are algorithms that group together data objects based on their similarities. Data scientists have a variety of so-called classifier algorithms that serve this purpose (see Glossary items, K-means algorith, K-nearest neighbor algorithm, Support vector machine). The so-called recommender algorithms that put individuals into predictable groups, based on the similarities of their preferences, might also be considered types of classifier algorithms (see Glossary items, Predictive analytics, Recommender). In addition, machine learning algorithms are sometimes referred to as classifiers, when they are intended to match similar objects based on some learned object attributes (see Glossary item, Machine learning). In all of such cases, the classifier algorithms group together similar items, but do not create a classification composed of related classes and subclasses. At the most, classifier algorithms provide data scientists with clues, from which a tentative classification can be constructed and tested.

Case Study 2.9: The Classification of Living Organisms

Many thousands of biologists have devoted much of their lives to the classification of living organisms. The relatively simple schema that constitutes the classification of life serves to drive down the complexity produced by millions of different species, all vying for their own unique existence. With this classification, all forms of life fall within a few dozen classes, and every class falls within a simple, hierarchical lineage (Figure 2.4).

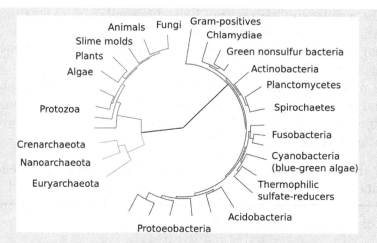

Figure 2.4 Modern classification of living organisms, a computer-generated schema indicating the hierarchical relationships among the major classes of living organisms [17]. Wikipedia, public domain.

Today, any high school student, spending a few moments to study the schema, can conjure a fairly good understanding of the major types of life on earth and their evolutionary relationships.

For the modern scientist, the classification of all living organisms has become the grand unifying theory of the biological sciences. Efforts to sequence the genomes of prokaryotic, eukaryotic, and viral species, thereby comparing the genomes of different classes of organisms, are driven by the classification; discoveries follow from questions that arise during its refinement. For example, in the case of infectious diseases, when scientists find a trait that informs us that what we thought was a single species is actually two species, it permits us to develop treatments optimized for each species, and to develop new methods to monitor and control the spread of both organisms. When we correctly group organisms within a common class, we can test and develop new drugs that are effective against all of the organisms within the class, particularly if those organisms are characterized by a molecule, pathway, or trait that is specifically targeted by a drug [18].

Much, if not all, of the perceived complexity of the biological sciences derives from the growing interconnectedness of once-separate disciplines: cell biology, ecology, evolution, climatology, molecular biology, pharmacology, genetics, computer sciences, paleontology, pathology, statistics, and so on. As once-isolated disciplines of science become entangled with one another, the classification of living organisms has been repurposed to tether these fields to their common subject matter: life.

Introspective Data—Data That Explains Itself

Introspection is a term borrowed from object-oriented programming. It refers to the ability of data (e.g., data records, documents, and other types of data objects) to describe itself when interrogated. Introspection gives data users the opportunity to see relationships among the individual data records that are distributed in different datasets.

Introspection is one of the most useful features of object-oriented programming languages. To illustrate, let us see how Ruby, a popular object-oriented programming language, implements introspection (see Glossary item, Object-oriented programming).

In Ruby, we can create a new object, "x," and assign it a string, such as "hello world."

$$x = \text{"hello world"}$$

Because the data object, "x," contains a string, Ruby knows that x belongs to the String class of objects. If we send the "class" method to the object, "x," Ruby will return a message indicating that "x" belongs to class String.

$$x.class \quad \text{yields String}$$

In Ruby, every object is automatically given an identifier (i.e., character string that is unique for the object). If we send the object the method "object_id," Ruby will tell us its assigned identifier.

$$x.object_id \quad \text{yields } 22502910$$

Ruby tells us that the unique object identifier assigned to the object "x" is 22502910.

In Ruby, should we need to learn the contents of "x," we can send the "inspect" method to the object. Should we need to know the methods that are available to the object, we can send the "methods" method to the object. All modern object-oriented languages support syntactic equivalents of these basic introspective tools (see Glossary item, Syntax).

The point of this short diversion into object-oriented programming is to demonstrate that modern programming languages allow the programmer to interrogate data and learn everything there is to know about the information contained in its data elements. Information about data objects, acquired during the execution of a program, can be used to modify a program's instructions, during run time, a useful feature known as "reflection" (see Glossary item, Reflection). Detailed information about every piece of data in a data set (e.g., the identifier associated with the data object, the class of objects to which the data object belongs, the data that the data object was created, the metadata and the data values that are associated with the data object), permit data scientists to integrate, relate, and repurpose data objects, stored on many different servers, at many different locations (see Glossary item, Data fusion, Data integration, Data merging, Metadata). Alas, most legacy data lacks introspection. Those who use legacy data must be prepared to expend a great deal of energy trying to understand the content and organization of the data [19].

REFERENCES

[1] Vogel HW. Monatsbericht der Konigl. Acad Wiss Berlin 1879.

[2] Huggins W. On the photographic spectra of stars. Phil Trans R Soc Lond 1880;171:669−90.

[3] A Review of the FBI's Handling of the Brandon Mayfield Case. U.S. Department of Justice, Office of the Inspector General, Oversight and Review Division, March 2006.

[4] Woese CR. Bacterial evolution. Microbiol Rev 1987;51:221−71.

[5] Woese CR, Fox GE. Phylogenetic structure of the prokaryotic domain: the primary kingdoms. PNAS 1977;74:5088−90.

[6] Beiko RG. Telling the whole story in a 10,000-genome world. Biol Direct 2011;6:34.

[7] Woese CR. Default taxonomy: Ernst Mayr's view of the microbial world. PNAS 1998;15. 1998;95(19):11043−46.

[8] Mayr E. Two empires or three? PNAS 1998;95:9720−3.

[9] Asimov I. Isaac Asimov Mulls "How do people get new ideas?" MIT Technol Rev. October 20, 2014.

[10] Berman JJ. Machiavelli's Laboratory. Seattle, WA: Amazon Digital Services, Inc.; 2010.

[11] Katsanis SH, Wagner JK. Characterization of the standard and recommended CODIS markers. J Forensic Sci 2012.

[12] Guessous I, Gwinn M, Khoury MJ. Genome-wide association studies in pharmacogenomics: untapped potential for translation. Genome Med 2009;1:46.

[13] McCarthy JJ, Hilfiker R. The use of single-nucleotide polymorphism maps in pharmacogenomics. Nat Biotechnol 2000;18:505−8.

[14] Nebert DW, Zhang G, Vesell ES. From human genetics and genomics to pharmacogenetics and pharmacogenomics: past lessons, future directions. Drug Metab Rev 2008;40:187−224.

[15] Personalised medicines: hopes and realities. The Royal Society, London, 2005. Available from: <https://royalsociety.org/~/media/Royal_Society_Content/policy/publications/2005/9631.pdf> [accessed 01.01.15].

[16] Klyne G, Newman C. Date and Time on the Internet: Timestamps. Network Working Group Request for Comments RFC:3339. Available from: <http://tools.ietf.org/html/rfc3339> [accessed 22.10.14].

[17] Letunic I, Bork P. Interactive tree of life (iTOL): an online tool for phylogenetic tree display and annotation. Bioinformatics 2007;23:127–8.

[18] Berman JJ. Taxonomic guide to infectious diseases: understanding the biologic classes of pathogenic organisms. Waltham, MA: Academic Press; 2012.

[19] Berman JJ. Principles of big data: preparing, sharing, and analyzing complex information. Burlington, MA: Morgan Kaufmann; 2013.

CHAPTER 3

Dealing with Text

3.1 THUS IT IS WRITTEN

It's only words, and words are all I have.

The Bee Gees

In a 2009 article, Keven Ashton wrote that most of the data that fills the Internet was created by humans, "by typing, pressing a record button, taking a digital picture, or scanning a bar code" [1]. We can be fairly confident that, at least for the foreseeable future, human-conceived text, with all of its poor orthography, poor grammar, and ill-conceived remarks, will be the primary source of data for repurposing projects. Within the aggregate of all textual data, seemingly composed by an army of monkeys banging away at keyboards, lies the collected wisdom of the human race.

Case Study 3.1: New Associations in Old Medical Literature

One of the purposes of reading is to discover new associations that link together diverse concepts, in unexpected ways. An example of a new and useful clinical association drawn from a simple search of the medical literature is Don Swanson's insight that fish oil may be helpful in the treatment of Raynaud's syndrome [2–4].

Raynaud's syndrome is a painful condition, typically involving the distal tips fingers or toes, and occurs in sensitive individuals who are exposed to cold. In Raynaud's syndrome, the vessels in affected tissues constrict, locally reducing the flow of oxygen. Searing pain may result, but the damage is seldom permanent, gradually reversing when the involved tissues are warmed. Don Swanson found several articles indicating that blood from individuals who suffered from Raynaud's syndrome had raised viscosity and reduced red blood cell deformability. This observation prompted Swanson to search the literature for substances that were known to reduce blood viscosity and increase red blood cell deformability. Fish oil was reputed to have these two properties, suggesting to Swanson that fish oil might be useful in the treatment of Raynaud's syndrome; and it was so. Swanson's success prompted Trevor Cohen and his coworkers to develop interactive software designed to find logical connections among concepts encountered in the medical literature [5].

If a book is a long sequence of words, ngrams are the subsequences of the book, and a complete collection of ngrams consists of all of the possible ordered subsequences of words in the text. Let's examine all the ngrams for the sequence,

"Ngrams are ordered word sequences."

Ngrams (1-gram)
are (1-gram)
ordered (1-gram)
word (1-gram)
sequences (1-gram)
Ngrams are (2-gram)
are ordered (2-gram)
ordered word (2-gram)
word sequences (2-gram)
Ngrams are ordered (3-gram)
are ordered word (3-gram)
ordered word sequences (3-gram)
Ngrams are ordered word (4-gram)
are ordered word sequences (4-gram)
Ngrams are ordered word sequences (5-gram)

Case Study 3.2: Ngram Analyses of Large Bodies of Text

Google has undertaken to enumerate the ngrams collected from scanned literature dating back to 1500. The public can enter their own ngrams into Google's ngram viewer, and receive a graph of the published occurrences of the phrase, through time.

For example, we can use Google's Ngram viewer to visualize the frequency of occurrence of the single word, "photon" (Figure 3.1).

The result fits into an historical narrative. The name "photon" comes from the Greek word for light. The word seems to have been used first in 1916, by Leonard T. Troland. When we chart the appearance of "photon" in published literature, we see that it does not appear until about 1920, when it entered common usage.

We can use the Ngram viewer to find trends (e.g., peaks, valleys, and periodicities) in data. Consider the Google Ngram Viewer results for the two-word ngram, "yellow fever" (Figure 3.2).

We see that the term "yellow fever" (a mosquito-transmitted hepatitis) appeared in the literature beginning about 1800 (shortly after an outbreak in Philadelphia), with several subsequent peaks (around 1915 and 1945). The dates of the peaks correspond roughly to outbreaks of yellow fever

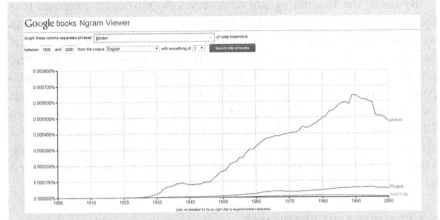

Figure 3.1 Google Ngram for the word "photon," from a corpus of literature covering 1900 to 2000. Notice that the first appearances of the term "photon" closely corresponds to its discovery, in the second decade of the twentieth century. Google Ngram viewer, with permission from Google.

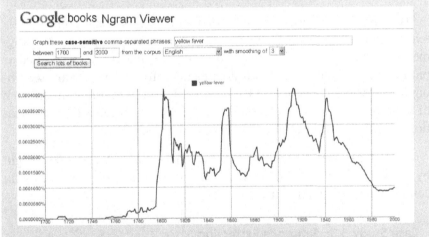

Figure 3.2 Google Ngram for the phrase "yellow fever," counting occurrences of the term in a large corpus, from the years 1700 to 2000. Peaks correspond to yellow fever epidemics. Google Ngram viewer, with permission from Google.

in Philadelphia (epidemic of 1793), New Orleans (epidemic of 1853), with U.S. construction efforts in the Panama Canal (1904–1914), and with well-documented WWII Pacific outbreaks (about 1942). Following the 1942 epidemic, an effective vaccine was available, and the incidence of yellow fever, as well as the literature occurrences of the "yellow fever" ngram, dropped precipitously. In this case, a simple review of ngram frequencies provides an accurate chart of historic yellow fever outbreaks.

By itself, the Google ngram data serves no particular purpose. It is the job of the imaginative data scientist to put the ngrams to work. As we have seen, ngrams can be used to document the invention of new concepts (e.g., the dawn of the quantum age), or to follow the emergence of epidemics. It is not hard to imagine that ngrams can be repurposed to trend cultural fads or cultural taboos. Google's own ngram viewer supports simple lookups of term frequencies. For more advanced analyses (e.g., finding co-occurrences of all ngrams against all other ngrams), data scientists can download the ngram data files, available at no cost from Google, and write their own programs, suited to their repurposing goals.

3.2 SEARCH AND RETRIEVAL

Knowledge can be public, yet undiscovered, if independently created fragments are logically related but never retrieved, brought together, and interpreted.
Donald R. Swanson [4]

Textual data analysis projects usually involve, at some point, simple search and retrieval routines. Sometimes, we search for specific fragments of text (i.e., a specific book or document, or a particular paragraph or sentence within a document). More often, we are searching for a chosen concept and its associated data, with the ultimate task of determining the relationship among a set of concepts (i.e., correlations, similarities, group membership, and so on).

Algorithms that search and retrieve concepts from text often begin by breaking text into sentences, the grammatic units that contain complete textual statements.

Case Study 3.3: Sentence Extraction

Many natural language algorithms attempt to derive sense from unstructured text (see Glossary item, Dark data). This involves parsing the text into sentences, and parsing sentences into assigned grammatic tokens (e.g., A = adjective, D = determiner, N = noun, P = preposition, V = main verb). A determiner is a word such as "a" or "the" that specifies the noun.

Consider the sentence, "The quick brown fox jumped over lazy dogs." This sentence can be grammatically tokenized as:

the::D
quick::A

brown::A
fox::N
jumped::V
over::P
the::D
lazy::A
dog::N

We can now express the sentence as the ordered sequence of its tokens: DAANVPDAN. This does not seem like much of a breakthrough, but imagine having a large collection of such token sequences representing every sentence from a large text corpus. With such a data set, we can observe the rules of sentence structure. Commonly recurring sequences, like DAANVPDAN, might be assumed to be proper sentences. Sequences that occur uniquely in a large text corpus are probably poorly constructed sentences. Before long, we might find ourselves constructing logic rules for reducing the complexity of sentences by dropping subsequences which, when removed, yield a sequence that occurs more commonly than the original sequence. For example, our table of sequences might indicate that we can convert DAANVPDAN into NVPAN (i.e., "Fox jumped over lazy dog"), without sacrificing too much of the meaning from the original sentence and preserving a grammatic sequence that occurs commonly in the text corpus.

This short example serves as an overly simplistic introduction to natural language processing. We can begin to imagine that the grammatic rules of a language can be represented by sequences of tokens which can be translated into words or phrases from a second language, and reordered according to grammatic rules appropriate to the target language.

Most natural language processing projects are repurposing projects. They involve translating text into something new or different (e.g., other languages, an index, a collection of names, a new text with words and phrases replaced with canonical forms extracted from a nomenclature).

All text processing projects begin by breaking pages and paragraphs into sentences. Computers have no way of knowing where one sentence begins and another starts, until the programmer provides a sentence parsing subroutine. There are many sentence parsing algorithms available. Perhaps the simplest method searches for a character pattern consisting of a sentence delimiter (i.e., a period) immediately following a lowercase alphabetic letter, and immediately preceding one or two space characters followed by an uppercase alphabetic character. For example:

"Here is a sentence. Here is another sentence."

Between the two sentences is the sequence "e. H," which consists of a lowercase "e" followed by a period followed by two spaces, followed by an uppercase "H." This general pattern (lowercase letter, period, one or two spaces, uppercase letter) usually signifies a sentence break. The pattern fails with sentences that break at the end of a line, or at the last sentence of a paragraph (i.e., where there is no intervening space). It also fails to demarcate proper sentences captured within one sentence (i.e., where a semicolon ends an expressed thought, but is not followed by an uppercase letter). It might falsely demarcate a sentence in an outline, where a lowercase letter is followed by a period, indicating a new, nonsentence subtopic. Nonetheless, with a few tweaks, a programmer can whip up an improved subroutine that divides unstructured text into a useful set of sentences.

Once we have our sentences, it is easy to pick out the terms contained in the sentence.

Case Study 3.4: Term Extraction

There's a big difference between knowing the name of something and knowing something.

Richard Feynman

Terms are the concepts within sentences. Consider the following:

"The diagnosis is chronic viral hepatitis."

This sentence contains two very specific medical concepts: "diagnosis" and "chronic viral hepatitis." These two concepts are connected to form a meaningful statement with the words "the" and "is," and the sentence delimiter, ".".

"The," "diagnosis," "is," "chronic viral hepatitis," ".".

A term can be defined as a sequence of one or more uncommon words that are demarcated (i.e., bounded on one side or another) by the occurrence of one or more common words, such as "is," "and," "with," "the." A list of such common words is referred to as a "stop list."

There are several available methods for finding and extracting index terms from a corpus of text [6], but no method is as simple, fast, and scalable as the "stop" word method [7]. Here is a step-by-step description of a very simple term extraction algorithm, using the "stop" method (see Glossary item, Term extraction algorithms):

1. Use the "stop list" published by the National Library of Medicine and shown here: "about, again, all, almost, also, although, always, among, an, and, another, any, are, as, at, be, because, been, before, being, between, both, but, by, can, could, did, do, does, done, due, during, each, either, enough, especially, etc., for, found, from, further, had, has, have, having, here, how, however, I, if, in, into, is, it, its, itself, just, kg, km, made, mainly, make, may, mg, might, ml, mm, most, mostly, must, nearly, neither, no, nor, obtained, of, often, on, our, overall, perhaps, pmid, quite, rather, really, regarding, seem, seen, several, should, show, showed, shown, shows, significantly, since, so, some, such, than, that, the, their, theirs, them, then, there, therefore, these, they, this, those, through, thus, to, upon, use, used, using, various, very, was, we, were, what, when, which, while, with, within, without, would."
2. Read the first word of the sentence. If it is a word found in the "stop list" delete the word from the sentence. If it is an uncommon word (i.e., not found in the "stop list"), save it.
3. Read the next word. If it is a common word, delete it, and place the saved word (from the prior step, if the prior step saved a word) into our list of terms found in the text. If it is an uncommon word, append it to the word we saved in step one, and save the 2-word term. If it is a sentence delimiter, place any saved term into our list of terms. Go to step 3.
4. If you've come to the end of the sentence, go to the next sentence, and start at step 2. Otherwise, repeat step 3.

This simple algorithm, or something much like it, is a fast and efficient method to build a collection of terms contained in a text corpus [8].

3.3 INDEXING TEXT

We must look for a long time before we can see.
Henry David Thoreau in "Natural History of Massachusetts"

Indexing seems to be a dying art. Individuals accustomed to electronic media tend to think of the Index as an inefficient or obsolete method for finding and retrieving information. Most currently available e-books have no index. It's far easier to pull up the "Find" dialog box and enter a word or phrase. The e-reader can find all matches quickly, providing the total number of matches, and bringing the reader to any or all of the pages containing the selection. This being the case, why should data scientists expend any effort on indexes (see Glossary item, Indexes)?

As an experiment, open an indexed book and read the index, from A to Z, as if you were reading the body of the text. You will find that the index refreshes your understanding of the concepts discussed in the book. The range of page numbers after each term indicates that a concept has extended its relevance across many different chapters. When you browse the different entries related to a single term, you begin to appreciate the versatility of the concepts contained in the book. **A well-designed index is a reconceptualization of the text that permits the book to be repurposed in ways that were not intended by the book's author.**

In prior decades and prior centuries, authors and editors devoted enormous effort into building indexes, sometimes producing multiple indexes for a single book. For example, a biography might contain a traditional alphabetized term index, followed by an alphabetized index of the names of the people included in the text. A zoology book might include an index specifically for animal names, with animals categorized according to their order within a biological classification. A geography index might list the names of localities subindexed by country, with countries subindexed by continent. In the past, a single book might have been annotated with extensive footnotes and supplemented with five or more indexes. In nineteenth century books, it was not unusual to publish indexes as stand-alone volumes (Figure 3.3).

You may be thinking that all this fuss over indexes is quaint, but it cannot apply to gigabyte and terabyte data sources. Actually, massive data resources that lack a proper index cannot be utilized to their full potential. Data by itself, even in large quantities, tells only part of a story. An index imposes order, simplicity, and meaning onto massive or complex data resources. Without an index, data resources can easily devolve into vast dumps of disorganized information. The best data indexes comply with international standards (i.e., ISO 999) and require creativity and professionalism [9]. Indexes should be accepted as another device for driving down the complexity of massive or complex data resources.

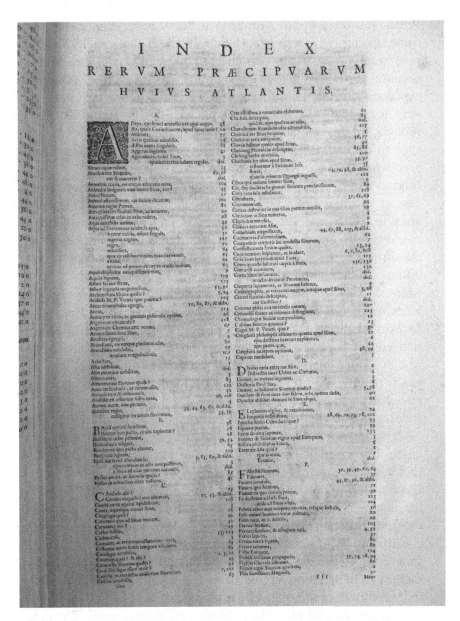

Figure 3.3 First page of Index to Novus Atlas Sinensis by Martino Martini, published in 1655, and scanned in Indiana University's Lilly Library. Wikipedia, public domain.

Here are a few of the specific strengths of an index that cannot be duplicated by "find" operations on terms entered into a query box:

1. An index can be read, like a book, to acquire a quick understanding of the contents and general organization of the data resource.

2. When you do a "find" search in a query box, your search may come up empty if there is nothing in the text that exactly matches your query. The index permits you to search subjects, without needing to know the exact wording in which the subject is expressed in the text (e.g., U.S., U.S.A., United States, and America should all point to the same pages).

3. Indexes are precompiled to contain the page numbers that are relevant to the index term. Hence, index searches are instantaneous, even when data corpus is enormous.

4. Indexes can be tied to a nomenclature or to a classification. In the case of an index tied to nomenclature, scientists can find the page links to all of the synonymous terms that fall under the same nomenclature entry (Section 3.4). In the case of an index tied to a classification, data scientists can determine relationships among different topics within the index, and within the text.

5. Many indexes are cross-indexed, providing relationships among index terms that might be extremely helpful to the data analyst.

6. Indexes for different data resources can be merged. When the location entries for index terms are annotated with the name of the resource, then merging indexes is trivial, and index searches will yield unambiguously identified locators in any of the data resources included in the merge.

7. Indexes can be created to satisfy a particular goal; and the process of creating a made-to-order index can be repeated again and again. For example, if you have a data resource devoted to ornithology, and you have an interest in the geographic location of species, you might want to create an index specifically keyed to localities, or you might want to add a locality subentry for every indexed bird name in your original index. Such indexes can be constructed as add-ons, when needed.

8. Indexes can be updated. If terminology or classifications change, there is nothing stopping you from redesigning and rebuilding the index, without modifying your primary data.

9. Indexes are created after the database has been created. The index can be designed to facilitate projects that repurpose the original data.

10. Indexes can serve as surrogates for the massive or complex data resource. In some cases, all the data user really needs is the index. A telephone book is an example of an index that serves its purpose without being attached to a related data source (e.g., caller logs, switching diagrams).

Case Study 3.5: Creating an Index

Once you have a method for extracting terms from sentences, the task of creating a true index, associating a list of locations with each term, is child's play for programmers. Short and simple programs for preparing indexes have been described [7]. Here is an simple description of an indexing program that operates on a text corpus:

1. Using term extraction software (described in Section 3.2), produce an alphabetized list of the terms contained in the text corpus.
2. Visually scan the list of terms, removing unwanted terms. This list will be the final list of terms in your index.
3. Write a simple software routine that parses through your text corpus sentence-by-sentence. Whenever a term from your index term list is encountered, your software will annotate the term, in the term list, with the location in the text corpus where the term was matched.
4. After the entire text has been parsed, you will have the list of terms you started with, wherein each term is followed by the ordered sequence of text locations where the term is matched. This is your index.

When the alphabetized list of terms is displayed, with each term followed by the ordered set of locations in the text where the term appears, then your index is completed! Computer-generated indexes are always somewhat crude, and are typically embellished and enhanced by professional indexers. If the size of the text is large (gigabytes or terabytes), then a simple index, such as the one described here, may suffice.

The most popular, and the most repurposed, index in the world today, is Google's PageRank index, used in every Google search.

Case Study 3.6: Ranking Search Results [10]

Page Rank (alternately, PageRank), is a computational method popularized by Google that searches through an index of every web page, to produce an ordered set of web pages whose content matches a query phrase. The rank of a page is determined by two scores: the relevancy of the page to the query phrase; and the importance of the page. The relevancy of the page is determined by factors such as how closely the text matches the query phrase, and whether the content of the page is focused on the subject of the query. The importance of the page is determined by how many Web pages link to and from the page, and the importance of the Web pages involved in the linkages. It is easy to see that the methods for scoring relevance and importance are subject to many algorithmic variances, particularly with respect to the choice of measures (i.e., the way in which a page's focus on a particular topic is quantified), and the weights applied to each measurement. The reasons that PageRank query responses can be completed rapidly is that the score of a page's importance is precomputed, and stored with the page's Web addresses. Word matches from the query phrase to Web pages are quickly assembled using a precomputed index of words, the pages containing the words, and the locations of the words in the pages [11].

Closely related to the concept of page ranking, is the concept of centrality. Centrality refers to a quantifier of the importance of an object among other objects. There is a large literature devoted to the various types of centrality and the many ways of measuring centrality. Most of the centrality algorithms are based on the assumption that something is of great central importance to other items if the other items to which it is connected are also important. In practical terms, this usually means that the centrality score of an object will be proportional to the centrality scores of the objects to which it is most similar.

Data repurposers, examining the U.S. Congressional Records, have used centrality measurements to identify the most influential members of the U.S. Senate [12], and mined the genetics literature to identify the likely gene-disease associations [13].

Of the many centrality methods available to data scientists, all seem to provide adequate quantifiers for the most central objects, but have limited success providing meaningful ranks to the less central objects. For example, consider your own experience with Google page rankings. You may find that the first dozen or so entries on the first page of a long list of query hits are just what you wanted. Once you get past the first dozen or so returns, you will find that the results quickly diminish in value. There may be no difference, in your own opinion, between the 30th hit and the 300th hit in terms of relevance to your search.

3.4 CODING TEXT

A synonym is a word you use when you can't spell the other one.

Baltasar Gracian.

A nomenclature is a specialized vocabulary, usually containing terms that comprehensively cover a well-defined field of knowledge. For example, there may be a nomenclature for diseases, or celestial bodies, or the makes and models of automobiles. Some nomenclatures are ordered alphabetically. Others are ordered by synonymy, wherein all synonyms and plesionyms (i.e., near-synonyms) are collected under a canonical (i.e., best or preferred) term (see Glossary items, Nomenclature mapping, Plesionymy, Thesaurus, Vocabulary). In many nomenclatures, grouped synonyms are collected under a code (unique alphanumeric string) assigned to the group. For example, in a tumor nomenclature, all of the synonyms for kidney cancer are assigned the same concept code C938500. The list of covered terms would include kidney cancer, kidney carcinoma, carcinoma of kidney, renal carcinoma, and a variety of equivalent arcane or less popular terms that lurk within a vast medical literature (e.g., hypernephroma, Grawitz tumor, and gurnistical tumor). Additional concept codes are used for biologically distinctive variants of kidney cancer (e.g., C6975300 → papillary variant of renal carcinoma, C4033000 → clear cell variant of renal carcinoma). Altogether, including variant concepts, there are over 550 nomenclature terms that express the concept of kidney cancer and its variants [14–17].

If you were to search a million medical documents for all records containing the specific term "kidney cancer" you would miss all the documents that contain the alternate equivalents, such as "carcinoma of kidney" or "renal carcinoma," and so on. It is easy to see that if a medical document were annotated with concept codes for every medical term included in the text, then a search through documents can collect all entries pertaining to a queried concept, regardless of which synonymous term actually appears in the text.

Nomenclatures have many purposes: to enhance interoperability and integration, to allow synonymous terms to be retrieved regardless of which specific synonym is entered as a query, to support comprehensive analyses of textual data, to express detail, to tag information in textual documents, and to drive down the complexity of documents by uniting synonymous terms under a common code. Sets of documents held in more than one massive or complex data resource can be harmonized under a nomenclature by substituting or appending a nomenclature code to every nomenclature term that appears in any of the documents. The task of assigning nomenclature codes to records within documents is referred to as "coding." If coding is done automatically, by a computer program, the process is known as "autocoding."

Assigning nomenclature codes to documents can be serious business. In the U.S., medical codes for diagnoses and therapeutic procedures are used for billing purposes, and mistakes have economic and legal consequences. Sometimes, medical coding directly effects the health and welfare of patients and their families. In 2009, the Department of Veterans Affairs sent out hundreds of letters to veterans with the devastating news that they had contracted Amyotrophic Lateral Sclerosis, also known as Lou Gehrig's disease, a fatal degenerative neurologic condition. About 600 of the recipients did not, in fact, have the disease. The VA retracted these letters, attributing the confusion to a coding error [18].

A popular approach to autocoding involves using the natural rules of language to find reasonable matches for grammatically equivalent terms. For example, the term "adenocarcinoma of lung" has much in common with alternate terms that have minor variations in word order, plurality, inclusion of articles, term splits by a word inserted for informational enrichment, and so on. Alternate forms would be "adenocarcinoma of the lung," "adenocarcinoma of the lungs," "lung adenocarcinoma," and "adenocarcinoma of the lung." A natural language algorithm takes into account grammatic variants, allowable alternate term constructions, word stems, and syntax variation (see Glossary item, Syntax). Clever improvements on natural language methods might include string similarity scores, intended to find term equivalences in cases for which grammatic methods come up short.

A limitation of the natural language approach to autocoding is encountered when synonymous terms lack etymologic commonality. Consider the term "submarine sandwich." Synonyms include "sub," "hoagie," "grinder," "hero," "torpedo," and "po' boy" are all synonyms for "submarine sandwich." All of these alternate terms are dissimilar from one another. Hence, there is no way to compute one synonym from any of the alternate forms. Data scientists are continually striving to develop improved algorithms for autocoders [19–21].

REFERENCES

[1] Ashton K. That "Internet of things" thing. RFID J 2009. Available from: <http://www.rfid-journal.com/articles/view?4986>; [accessed 16.11.14].

[2] Swanson DR. Fish oil, Raynaud's syndrome, and undiscovered public knowledge. Perspect Biol Med 1986;30:7–18.

[3] Swanson DR. Medical literature as a potential source of new knowledge. Bull Med Libr Assoc 1990;78:29–37.

[4] Swanson DR. Undiscovered public knowledge. Libr Q 1986;56:103–18.

[5] Cohen T, Whitfield GK, Schvaneveldt RW, Mukund K, Rindflesch T. EpiphaNet: an interactive tool to support biomedical discoveries. J Biomed Discov Collab 2010;5:21–49.

[6] Krauthammer M, Nenadic G. Term identification in the biomedical literature. J Biomed Inform 2004;37:512–26.

[7] Berman JJ. Methods in medical informatics: fundamentals of healthcare programming in perl, python, and ruby. Boca Raton, FL: Chapman and Hall; 2010.

[8] Berman JJ. Automatic extraction of candidate nomenclature terms using the doublet method. BMC Med Inform Decis Mak 2005;5:35.

[9] Wallis E, Lavell C. Naming the indexer: where credit is due. Indexer 1995;19:266–8.

[10] Berman JJ. Principles of big data: preparing, sharing, and analyzing complex information. Burlington, MA: Morgan Kaufmann; 2013.

[11] Brin S, Page L. The anatomy of a large-scale hypertextual Web search engine. Comput Networks ISDN Syst 1998;33:107–17.

[12] Fader A, Radev D, Crespin MH, Monroe BL, Quinn KM, Colaresi KM. MavenRank: identifying influential members of the US senate using lexical centrality. In: Proceedings of the joint conference on empirical methods in natural language processing and computational natural language learning (EMNLP-CoNLL), Prague, Czech Republic. 2007. p. 658–66.

[13] Ozgur A, Vu T, Erkan G, Radev DR. Identifying gene-disease associations using centrality on a literature mined gene-interaction network. Bioinformatics 2008;24:i277–85.

[14] Berman JJ. Tumor taxonomy for the developmental lineage classification of neoplasms. BMC Cancer 2004;4:88 <http://www.biomedcentral.com/1471-2407/4/88>; [accessed 01.01.15].

[15] Berman JJ. Modern classification of neoplasms: reconciling differences between morphologic and molecular approaches. BMC Cancer 2005;5:100. Available from: <http://www.biomed-central.com/1471-2407/5/100>; [accessed 01.01.15].

[16] Berman JJ. Tumor classification: molecular analysis meets Aristotle. BMC Cancer 2004;4:10. Available from: <http://www.biomedcentral.com/1471-2407/4/10>; [accessed 01.01.15].

[17] Berman JJ. Neoplasms: principles of development and diversity. Sudbury, ON: Jones & Bartlett; 2009.

[18] Hayes A. VA to apologize for mistaken Lou Gehrig's disease notices. CNN; 2009. Available from: <http://www.cnn.com/2009/POLITICS/08/26/veterans.letters.disease>; [accessed 04.09.12].

[19] Berman JJ. Doublet method for very fast autocoding. BMC Med Inform Decis Mak 2004;4:16.

[20] Berman JJ. Resources for comparing the speed and performance of medical autocoders. BMC Med Inform Decis Mak 2004;4:8.

[21] Berman JJ. Nomenclature-based data retrieval without prior annotation: facilitating biomedical data integration with fast doublet matching. In Silico Biol 2005;5:0029.

CHAPTER 4

New Life for Old Data

4.1 NEW ALGORITHMS

Today, most software exists, not to solve a problem, but to interface with other software.

IO Angell

Case Study 4.1: Lunar Orbiter Image Recovery Project

Following the first manned Apollo mission to the moon (Apollo 11, July 20, 1969), the five subsequent Apollo missions left behind recording instruments on the lunar surface. The collective set of downlinked data received from these instruments is known as the Apollo Lunar Surface Experiments Package (ALSEP). More than 11,000 data tapes were recorded.

During the Apollo program, control and use of the tapes, as well as the responsibility to safely archive the tapes, was transferred among various agencies and institutions. When the Apollo mission ended, funds were low, and a portion of the data that had been distributed to various investigators and agencies was never sent to the official archives [1]. It should come as no surprise that, at the present time, about half of the ALSEP tapes are missing; their whereabouts uncertain. Of the available tapes, much of the data is difficult to access, due to the use of abandoned data media (i.e., 7 and 9 track tapes) and obsolete data formats [1] (see Glossary item, Abandonware) (Figures 4.1 and 4.2).

Available ALSEP data, when converted into a modern data format, has proven to be a valuable asset, when reanalyzed with new analytic tools. For example, the first analyses of ALSEP's seismic data, conducted 35 years ago, indicated that about 1300 deep moonquakes had occurred during the period when the data was being downlinked. The field of seismic analysis has advanced in the interim. A reanalysis of the same data, using modern techniques, has produced an upward revision of the first estimate; to about 7000 deep moonquakes [1].

Figure 4.1 Earth's first view of itself, from a location near the moon, by the United States Lunar Orbiter I, on August 23, 1966. U.S. National Aeronautics and Space Administration (NASA), public domain.

Figure 4.2 Same image as shown in Figure 4.1, but processed and enhanced by NASA. NASA, public domain.

Today, there is a renewed push to find, collect, and archive the missing ALSEP data. Why is there a sudden urgency to finish a chore that should have been completed decades ago? Simply put, the tapes must be restored before the last of the original investigators, who alone understand the scope and organization of the data, vanish into retirement or death.

Case Study 4.2: Finding New Planets from Old Data

Astronomers gather enormous amounts of information on stars. Such data includes direct photographic images of stars, using improved telescopes (e.g., Hubble Space Telescope), high-resolution spectroscopy data, X-ray data (e.g., from NASA's Chandra X-ray observatory). As it happens, if a star is orbited by planets, those planets will have some effect, over the course of time, on the measurements collected on the star [2].

Currently, using preexisting star data, astronomers have found evidence for nearly 2000 extrasolar planets (exoplanets). Some of the planet-hunting techniques include [2]:

- Transit method. Exoplanets dim the light received from a star during their transit.
- Radial velocity or Doppler method. Exoplanets can cause the star's speed to vary with respect to the speed at which the star moves towards or away from the earth, and this variation in speed causes a Doppler shift in the star's emitted spectral lines.
- Transit timing variation. If a star is orbited by multiple planets, then the time when an exoplanet begins its transit across the star, and the duration of its transit, will vary, depending on the other planets in the vicinity at the time of transit.
- Gravitational microlensing. Exoplanets orbiting a lensing star can produce perturbations in the measured magnification of the lensing phenomenon.
- Astrometry. Orbiting exoplanets can change the star's position in the sky.
- Pulsar timing. Orbiting exoplanets may cause small perturbations in the timing of radio wave pulsations. This method, which applies only to planets orbiting pulsars, was employed to find the first confirmed exoplanet, in 1992.
- Direct imaging. When the exoplanets are large, and the star is relatively close to the earth, the exoplanets can be imaged directly, by blocking the light produced by their star (see Figure 4.3).

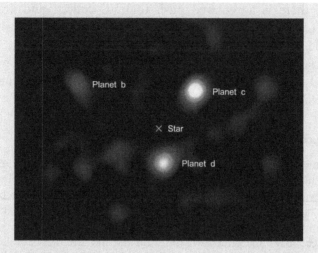

Figure 4.3 Direct imaging of three exoplanets orbiting HR8799, 120 light years from earth, was obtained. The orbiting exoplanets were made visible in the image, by blocking out the image of their star. NASA, obtained with the Palomar Observatory's Hale Telescope, public domain.

Today, new methods for finding exoplanets are being developed. Existing data is being repurposed to accommodate the newest techniques. Data that has already been used to find exoplanets is being reanalyzed to help find additional planets missed in the first analysis, or to uncover new information about exoplanets that have been discovered [3].

Data modeling is a method whereby data sets, or the relations of variables within data sets, can be expressed by mathematical formulae or by semantic notation (see Glossary items, Semantics, Variable). It sometimes happens that a data model hits upon a fundamental law that helps us to understand how the universe operates. For example, repeated measurements of force, mass, and acceleration observed on moving bodies might produce a formula that applies consistently, at any time, any place, and with any object (i.e., $f = ma$). Miracles aside, most data models are, at best, ways of simplifying sets of measurements. Data models often provide no real understanding of how systems work, and cannot always be relied upon to usefully predict the behavior of a system over time.

Case Study 4.3: New but Ultimately Wrong: Market Prediction

Recent experience with the Gaussian copula function provides a cautionary tale [4]. This formerly honored and currently vilified formula, developed for

Wall Street, was used to calculate the risk of default correlation (i.e., the likelihood that two investment vehicles would default together) based on the current market value of the vehicles, and without factoring in historical data (see Glossary item, Correlation distance). The formula was easy to implement, and became a favorite model for predicting risk in the securitization market. Though the Gaussian copula function had its early detractors, it soon became the driving model on Wall Street. In about 2008, the function simply stopped working (see Glossary item, Nongeneralizable predictor). Then came the 2008 market collapse. In some circles, the Gaussian copula function is blamed for the global economic disaster [5].

As algorithms become more and more clever, they become more and more enigmatic. Fewer and fewer people truly understand how they work. Some of the most enduring statistical methods defy simple explanation, sometimes producing inscrutable or irreproducible results (see Glossary items, Linear regression, *P*-value, Overfitting) [6–8]. Newer techniques, geared to answer questions that classic statistics cannot handle, are likewise problematic. Much of modern data analytics involves combinatorics, the evaluation, on some numeric level, of combinations of things. Such evaluations might include pairwise comparisons of data objects based on distance or some other measurement (see Glossary, Euclidean distance). The goal of these comparisons often involves clustering data into similar groups, finding relationships among data that will lead to classifying the data objects, or predicting how data objects will respond or change under a particular set of conditions. When the number of comparisons becomes large, the time required to complete a set of calculations can become too long to tolerate. For this reason, data scientists are always on the look-out for innovative noncombinatoric solutions for traditionally combinatoric problems.

Sometimes the best recourse for the data scientist is to repurpose the available data to produce better, simpler metrics; not better algorithms.

Case Study 4.4: Choosing Better Metrics

Sabermetrics is a sterling example of analysis using simple metrics that are chosen to correlate well with a specific outcome; a winning ball game. In the past several decades, baseball analysts have developed a wide variety of new performance measurements for baseball players. These include: base runs, batting average on balls in play, defense-independent pitching statistics, defense-independent earned run average, fielding independent pitching, total player rating, or batter—fielder wins, total pitcher index, and ultimate zone rating. Most of these metrics were developed empirically, tested in the field, literally, and optimized as needed. They are all simple linear metrics that use combinations of weighted measures on data collected during ballgames. Though sabermetrics has its detractors, everyone would agree that it represents a fascinating and largely successful effort to bring objective numeric techniques to the field of baseball. Nothing in sabermetrics involves so-called "deep" analytic techniques (see Glossary item, Deep analytics). Sabermetric techniques rely on simple metrics, developed from a savvy appreciation of the game of baseball, that can be easily calculated and validated.

4.2 TAKING CLOSER LOOKS

Man needs more to be reminded than instructed.

Samuel Johnson

One of the most important uses of legacy data is to tell us when we are wrong. Expert judgment is sometimes poor judgment, built on "confirmation bias," wherein the expert forms an hypothesis, and then interprets all new observations to fit his original hypothesis, never actually testing its truth (see Glossary item, Negative study bias).

Case Study 4.5: Expertise Is No Substitute for Data Analysis

If you are a fan of the television show Crime Scene Investigation, then you must know that a cracked hyoid bone (the U-shaped neck bone that lies above the thyroid cartilage) is a sure sign of strangulation. The association between strangulation and cracked hyoid is so often repeated that we can all assume that all cases of strangulation will result in a broken hyoid bone. Not so. Strangulation results from a closure of the throat, caused by the exertion of external pressure, and may occur in the absence of a fractured hyoid.

In South Carolina, three murders occurred in which the victims were strangled, but their hyoid bones were not cracked. Without delving into the details of the case, it happens that the prosecution needed to determine whether the murders were committed by one person, or by several different persons. Forensic pathologists who examined these cases insisted that strangulations without hyoid fractures were extremely rare. The experts reasoned that three strangulations, in the same geographic region, without hyoid fractures, were so unlikely that they must have all been perpetrated by one criminal, using a unique murder method.

Unswayed by the opinion of experts, data analysts found a new purpose for old autopsy reports: producing an objective determination of the frequency of occurrence of strangulations with or without hyoid bone fracture. Review of cases in the autopsy database revealed that strangulation without hyoid fracture is common; not rare. The experts had relied on their subjective, and mistaken, perception that strangulation without hyoid fracture is rare. Subsequent review of the crime scenes of the three murders uncovered many differences in the circumstances and evidentiary findings, from case to case. Had the experts relied more on data than on their collective memories, they may have concluded that more than one perpetrator may have been responsible for the three murders [9].

In the past decade, some of the fundamental assumptions of forensic science have been challenged [10,11]. Following the 2004 terrorist bombings of railways in Madrid, Spain, FBI experts linked a partial set of incriminating fingerprints to a U.S. citizen, who was promptly arrested. Multiple experts reviewed the case and agreed that the fingerprints positively identified the suspect. Everyone was confident that the perpetrator of the bombings was in custody. Some weeks later, the same set of fingerprints were used to identify another man, with known terrorist connections [12]. The original suspect was released.

We now know that the science of fingerprint matching is not perfect. Similarly, some of the most entrenched methods in fire investigation have been shown to lack firm scientific basis [13,14].

When there is suspicion that systemic mistakes have occurred over a long period of time, old records should be reviewed and repurposed. Legal records (e.g., criminal cases, medical records, financial transactions) are collected for the purpose of successfully completing an activity at hand (e.g., arresting a criminal, treating a patient, completing a banking transaction). After the data has been collected, the aggregate collection can be used to check whether systemic errors were made, whether basic assumptions were justified, and whether the stories we told ourselves at the start of the data collection are the same as the stories we learned from the old data.

Case Study 4.6: Life on Mars

On September 3, 1976, the Viking Lander 2 landed on the planet mars, where it remained operational for the next 3 years, 7 months and 8 days. Soon after landing, it performed an interesting remote-controlled experiment. Using samples of martian dirt, astrobiologists measured the conversion of radioactively-labeled precursors into more complex carbon-based molecules; the so-called Labeled-Release study. For this study, control samples of dirt were heated to a high temperature (i.e., sterilized), and likewise exposed to radioactively-labeled precursors, without producing complex carbon-containing molecules. The tentative conclusion, published soon thereafter, was that Martian organisms residing within the samples of dirt had built carbon-based molecules through a metabolic pathway [15]. As you might expect, the conclusion was immediately challenged, and remains controversial to this day, nearly 32 years later.

In the years since 1976, long after the initial conclusions were published, the data from the Labeled-Release study has been made available to scientists, for reanalysis. New analytic techniques have been applied to the data, and new interpretations have been published [15]. As additional missions have reached mars, more data has emerged (i.e., the detection of water and methane), also supporting the conclusion that there is life on mars. None of the data is conclusive, because Martian organisms have not been isolated. The point made here is that the Labeled-Release data is accessible and permanent, and can be studied again and again, compared to or combined with new data, and disputed ad nauseam.

Most people would agree that the simple act of counting data is something that can be done accurately and reproducibly, from laboratory to laboratory (see Glossary item, Reproducibility). Actually, this is not so. Some of the most useful scientific advances have involved improved methods for counting data objects.

Case Study 4.7: The Number of Human Chromosomes

One of the basic facts of biology is that the so-called normal complement of chromosomes in human diploid cells is 46. Most people living today are unaware that until 1955, the scientifically accepted number of chromosomes in human cells was 48. Until that time, the standard chromosome count was based on bad counting technique. There must have been some biologists who did their own count, coming up with the correct number (i.e., 46), but disputes in science are typically settled in favor of the reigning paradigm.

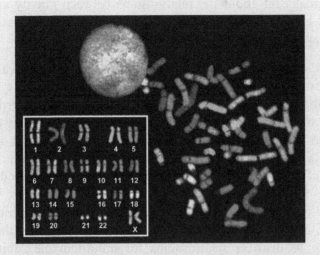

Figure 4.4 Spectral karyotype (i.e., chromosome spread) of a human female cell. Spectral karyotyping involves in situ *hybridization of DNA against fluorescent probes specific for individual chromosomes. The top object is the nucleus. To the left are the spread chromosomes prepared from a cell undergoing mitosis. The inset shows the aligned pairs of chromosomes, positioned for easy examination.* National Human Genome Research Institute, Institutes of Health, Talking Glossary of Genetic Terms, public domain.

In 1955, a better method of chromosome counting was discovered. Treatment of cells with colchicine arrested mitotic activity at a point where the chromosomes were optimally extended. At about the same time, it was found that spreading the chromosomes in a hypotonic saline solution helped to separate one chromosome from another. Hence, in 1955, chromosome counts were conducted in a manner that could not be contested [16]. Anyone, in any lab, could perform superb chromosome spreads, accurately count the chromosomes, and satisfy themselves that the number of chromosomes was 46; not 48 (Figure 4.4).

4.3 CROSSING DATA DOMAINS

Nobody goes there anymore. It's too crowded.

Yogi Berra

We are raised to believe that science explains how the universe, and everything in it, works. Engineering and the other applied sciences use scientific explanations to create things, for the betterment of our world. This is a lovely way to think about the roles played by scientists and engineers, but it is not accurate. For the most part, we do not know very much about the universe. Nobody understands the true nature of gravity, or mass, or light, or magnetism, or atoms, or thought. We do know a great deal about the relationships between gravity and mass, mass and energy, energy and light, light and magnetism, atoms and mass, thought and neurons, and so on.

Here is an example of a mathematical relationship that we know to be true, but which defies our understanding. The constant pi is the ratio of the circumference of a circle to its diameter. Furthermore, pi figures into the Gaussian statistical distribution (i.e., that describes how a normal population is spread). How is it possible that a number that determines the distribution of a population can also determine the diameter of a circle [17]? The relationships are provable and undeniable, but the full meaning of pi is beyond our grasp. We are comfortable using equations that describe the actions and properties of one thing, in terms of the actions or properties of another thing. It is our ability to discover relationships for unfathomable subjects that enables us to describe how the universe behaves, and to construct new objects with useful and predictable properties.

Things that seem unrelated may be related if we just think about them. For example, astrology is dismissed because it is obvious that distant heavenly bodies play no rule in the course of human events. But, we know that the position of the moon relative to the earth causes the tides, and that the tides can have profound effects here on earth. We encounter a large number of events that are influenced by the position of the sun relative to the earth (e.g., day and night, winter and summer). Perhaps the position of venus may influence bird migration patterns, or an ancient supernova may have influenced crucial events in the emergence of life on earth. The point here is that finding relationships, just like any other scientific endeavor, requires the thoughtful analysis of data. We never know until we look.

Examples of the kinds of relationships that might be examined in data repurposing projects could include:

- Dollar migration patterns and the geographic spread of a flu epidemic
- Cellphone traffic and traffic jams
- Lamp-post breakages and high-crime localities
- Cancer deaths and socio-economic status
- Death certificate completeness and quality of care
- National salt intake and deaths caused by hypertension
- Height of mountains and drought conditions [18].

The creative data scientist looks for new connections between apparently unrelated data sets.

Case Study 4.8: Linking Global Warming to High-Intensity Hurricanes

The UK Hadley Centre maintains a database of sea surface temperatures, over a 5° latitude–longitude global grid, from the year 1850, to the present (see Glossary item, Grid) [19]. This data tells us how the ocean temperature changes seasonally and geographically, over time. Kerry Emanuel found a new use for the Hadley data when he noticed an association between regionally increased ocean temperatures and particularly strong hurricanes spawned in these same regions. Reviewing 50 years of data, Emanuel confirmed that the intensity of hurricanes increased in step with the warming of the North Atlantic and Pacific oceans [20]. A data set, intended primarily for charting trends in water temperature and correlating those trends with the oceanic reach of sea ice, found a new use: forecasting the intensity of hurricanes.

It is human nature to evaluate the world through direct observations. If we want to know the length of an object, we measure its length with a ruler. If we want to know the number of eggs in a basket, we count the eggs. If we are clever, we can determine the height of an object by comparing the length of its shadow, with the length of the shadow of an object of known height. We can estimate the number of eggs in a basket by weighing the basket, with and without the eggs, and dividing the total weight of the eggs by the predetermined average weight of a single egg. When we have a wealth of descriptive data about many different objects in our environment, we can find new ways to evaluate our world, without making new measurements.

Case Study 4.9: Inferring Climate Trends with Geologic Data

Mountains are like icebergs made of rock. The bulk of a mountain is buried underground. When the top of the mountain is eroded, the weight of the mountain is reduced, and the mountain bobs upwards, a little bit. The natural process through which mountains are flattened, over eons, requires the erosion of its surface plus its ever-rising subsurface.

When water is sucked from a mountain, the mountain lightens and rises. Likewise, if the water is sucked out of a tectonic plate, the entire plate (i.e., the surface of the planet overlying the plate) will rise. The National Science Foundation's Plate Boundary Observatory provides precise measurements of ground positions from data generated by GPS

(Global Positioning System) satellites. A group of scientists working at the Scripps Institution of Oceanography found that all of the ground stations in the western U.S. exhibited measurable uplift. In the period 2003–2004, the western states rose an average of 0.15 in, and the western mountains rose more than half an inch in the same period. This wide rise coincides with a long drought in the west. It would seem that the only explanation for the uplift of the tectonic plate, and the greater uplift of the western mountains, is the loss of water, via evaporation, without replacement. So strong is the relationship between water loss and mountain rise that water resources in the west can now be tracked with GPS ground measurements [18].

Sometimes, the data scientist must travel back in time, to understand mysteries that persist into the present.

Case Study 4.10: Old Tidal Data, and the Iceberg that Sank the Titanic [4]

A recent headline story explains how century old tidal data plausibly accounts for the iceberg that sank the titanic, on April 15, 1912 [21]. Old records show that several months earlier, in 1912, the moon earth and sun aligned to produce a strong tidal pull, and this happened when the moon was the closest it had come to the earth in 1,400 years. The resulting tidal surge was sufficient to break the January Labrador ice sheet, sending a large number of icebergs towards the open North Atlantic waters. The Labrador icebergs arrived in the commercial shipping lanes 4 months later, in time for a fateful rendezvous with the Titanic. Back in January 1912, when tidal measurements were being collected, nobody foresaw that the data would be repurposed a century later.

REFERENCES

[1] Recovering the missing ALSEP data. Solar System Exploration Research Virtual Institute. NASA. Available from: <http://sservi.nasa.gov/articles/recovering-the-missing-alsep-data/>; [accessed 13.10.14].

[2] Bracewell RN, MacPhie RH. Searching for non solar planets. Icarus 1979;38:136–47.

[3] Khan A. Possible earth-like planets could hold water: scientists cautious. Los Angeles Times; 2012.

[4] Berman JJ. Principles of Big Data: Preparing, Sharing, and Analyzing Complex Information. Burlington, MA: Morgan Kaufmann; 2013.

[5] Salmon F. Recipe for disaster: the formula that killed wall street. Wired Magazine 17:03, 2009.

[6] Cohen J. The earth is round ($p < .05$). Am Psychol 1994;49:997–1003.

[7] Janert PK. Data analysis with open source tools. Sebastopol, CA: O'Reilly Media; 2010.

[8] Nuzzo R. P values, the gold standard of statistical validity, are not as reliable as many scientists assume. Nature 2014;506:150–2.

[9] Safarik M, Ramsland K. Clinical judgment vs. data analysis. Forensic Exam 2012;21:14–19.

[10] Strengthening forensic science in the United States: a path forward. The Committee on Identifying the Needs of the Forensic Science Community and the Committee on Science, Technology, and Law Policy and Global Affairs and the Committee on Applied and Theoretical Statistics, Division on Engineering and Physical Sciences. Washington, DC: The National Academies Press; 2009.

[11] Tonry M. Learning from the limitations of deterrence research. Crime Justice 2008;37:279–311.

[12] A review of the FBI's handling of the brandon mayfield case. US Department of justice, office of the inspector general, oversight and review division, 2006.

[13] Tanner R. New science challenges arson conviction. New York, NY: Associated Press; 2006.

[14] Lentini JJ. Scientific protocols for fire investigation. Boca Raton, FL: CRC Press; 2006 [chapter 8].

[15] Bianciardi G, Miller JD, Straat PA, Levin GV. Complexity analysis of the viking labeled release experiments. Int J Aeronaut Space Sci 2012;13:14–26.

[16] Tjio TH, Levan A. The chromosome number of man. Hereditas 1956;42:1–6.

[17] Wigner E. The unreasonable effectiveness of mathematics in the natural sciences. Communications in pure and applied mathematics, vol. 13. New York, NY: John Wiley and Sons; 1960.

[18] Borsa AA, Agnew DC, Cayan DR. Ongoing drought-induced uplift in the western United States. Science 2014.

[19] CISL Research Data Archive. <http://rda.ucar.edu/datasets/ds277.3/>; [accessed 08.11.14].

[20] Roush W. The gulf coast: a victim of global warming? Technol Rev 2005.

[21] Forsyth J. What sank the Titanic? Scientists point to the moon. Reuters 2012.

CHAPTER 5

The Purpose of Data Analysis Is to Enable Data Reanalysis

5.1 EVERY INITIAL DATA ANALYSIS ON COMPLEX DATASETS IS FLAWED

I visited the Sage of reverend fame
And thoughtful left more burden'd than I came.
I went—and ere I left his humble door
The busy World had quite forgot his name.

Ecclesiastes

It is difficult to perform any complex task correctly, on the first try. If you doubt this claim, consider some recent titles of scientific reviews that evaluate the reliability of published research.

1. **"Unreliable research: Trouble at the lab"** [1]. *The Economist*, in 2013, ran an article examining flawed biomedical research. The magazine article referred to an NIH official who indicated that "researchers would find it hard to reproduce at least three-quarters of all published biomedical findings, the public part of the process seems to have failed." The article also described a study conducted at the pharmaceutical company Amgen, wherein 53 landmark studies were repeated. The Amgen scientists were successful at reproducing the results of only 6 of the 53 studies. Another group, at Bayer HealthCare, repeated 63 studies. The Bayer group succeeded in reproducing the results of only one-fourth of the original studies.
2. **"A decade of reversal: An analysis of 146 contradicted medical practices"** [2]. The authors reviewed 363 journal articles, reexamining established standards of medical care. Among these articles were 146 manuscripts (40.2%) claiming that an existing standard of care had no clinical value (see Glossary item, Meta-analysis).
3. **"Cancer fight: Unclear tests for new drug"** [3]. This *New York Times* article examined whether a common test performed on breast cancer tissue (Her2) was repeatable. It was shown that for patients who tested positive for Her2, a repeat test indicated that 20% of the original positive assays were actually negative (i.e., falsely positive on the initial test) [3].

4. **"Why most published research findings are false"** [4]. Modern scientists often search for small effect sizes, using a wide range of available analytic techniques, and a flexible interpretation of outcome results. Under such conditions, the manuscript author found that research conclusions are more likely to be false than true [4].

Experiments need to be validated (see Glossary item, Validation). As it happens, it is difficult to repeat a complex experiment. In many instances, the best we can hope for is to reanalyze the original experiment, to verify that the data was obtained properly and to validate that the conclusions fit the results. Reanalysis is important because it is difficult to analyze a complex study correctly, on the first try. For creative data scientists, reanalysis is more important than the primary analysis, because it provides them with an opportunity to reimagine the meaning and the purpose of the data. For society, reanalysis provides the public with a way to set things right.

When trying to understand why so many scientific studies are non-reproducible, it helps to divide potential errors into three categories:

1. Preanalytic (e.g., errors in experimental design, data measurement, data collection)
2. Analytic (e.g., errors in data filtering, data transformation, choice of statistical or analytic tests, execution of tests)
3. Postanalytic (e.g., errors in the interpretation of results).

Examples of all three types of reproducibility errors abound in the scientific literature.

Case Study 5.1: Sample Mix-Ups, a Preanalytic Error

The journal *Nature* published an interesting article, under the droll banner, "Agony for researchers as mix-up forces retraction of ecstasy study" [5]. It seems that scientists at the Johns Hopkins University School of Medicine had reported in the journal *Science* that the drug ecstasy, in small doses, damaged dopamine-producing brain cells in monkeys. This observation fit the authors' original hypothesis that ecstasy is a neurotoxin. As it turned out, the Johns Hopkins scientists were obliged to retract their original article when it was determined that the wrong drug had been injected, by mistake, during the experiment (i.e., no ecstasy; just agony) [5].

Huntington disease is associated with a repeated trinucleotide occurring in a specific chromosome region (i.e., the CAG repeat). In a review of over 1,000 persons with Huntington disease, 30 were found to lack the diagnostic CAG repeat. 18 of these 30 cases were accounted for by misdiagnosis, sample mix-up, or clerical error [6]. Likewise, anomalous and impossible results have been obtained from DNA sequence analyses of mitochondria. Laboratories were reporting examples wherein a single individual was shown to have multiple ancestries; a biological impossibility. Sample mix-up and sample contamination (from other specimens) were demonstrated in these cases [7,8].

Sample mix-ups are not rare [9]. In 2010, the UK National Health Services reported 800,000 organ donor list errors among a database of 14 million records [10]. The potential errors would include instances wherein a donor listed a particular organ intended for removal, whereas some other organ would have been removed, when the time came. It happens.

Reanalysis is a never-ending process that supports multiple iterations. After a successful reanalysis, why not reanalyze the reanalysis?

Case Study 5.2: Vanishing Exoplanets: An Analytic Error

We have previously seen a case study wherein exoplanets were discovered by repurposing data collected by the U.S. National Aeronautics and Space Administration's Chandra x-ray observatory (see Section 4.1). As an exoplanet transits a star, it focally blocks the x-rays emitted by the star. Searchers for new exoplanets scan for dips in x-ray emissions, consistent with the transit of an exoplanet.

Early data that confirmed the discovery of new exoplanets were reanalyzed, this time taking into account effects of the magnetic field produced by rotating stars [11]. In the reanalysis study, the author found that certain stars could produce a periodic Doppler shift that modulated the intensity of x-ray emissions. The M dwarf star Gliese 581 had been reported to host four exoplanets. When the authors corrected for Doppler shift, two of the four planets vanished.

Initial studies tend to exaggerate their own importance. This is part of human nature and will never change. Reanalyses tend to take some of the air out of overinflated primary studies. In this case, two planets were evaporated. Not to be overlooked, the reanalysis verified the existence of the remaining two planets and confirmed that the original study was substantially correct. Perhaps, more importantly, the reanalysis improved our ability to identify true exoplanets, by providing a method that effectively boosts our detection of blocked x-ray signals, by compensating for a Doppler effect that would otherwise reduce signals.

At the height of the cold war, the story was told of a foot race between Russia's fastest runner and American's fastest runner. As the story is told, the American won. A Russian newspaper reported the outcome under the following headline banner: "In International race, Russia comes in second! Struggling American comes in next to last." Strictly speaking, the headline was correct, but the postanalytic interpretation was biased and misleading.

The most common source of scientific errors is postanalytic, arising from the interpretation of results [4,12–16]. Preanalytic errors and analytic errors, though common, are much less frequently encountered than interpretation errors. Virtually every journal article contains, hidden in the Introduction and Discussion sections, some distortion of fact or misleading assertion. Scientists cannot be objective about their own work. As humans, we tend to interpret observations to reinforce our beliefs and prejudices and to advance our agendas.

One of the most common strategies whereby scientists distort their own results, to advance a self-serving conclusion, is message framing [17]. In message framing, scientists omit from discussion any pertinent findings that might diminish or discredit their own conclusions. The common practice of message framing is conducted on a subconscious, or at least a subrational, level. A scientist is not apt to read articles whose conclusions contradict his own hypotheses, and he will not cite disputatious works in his manuscripts. Furthermore, if a paradigm is held in high esteem by a majority of the scientists in a field, then works that contradict the paradigm are not likely to pass peer review. Hence, it is difficult for contrary articles to be published in scientific journals. In any case, the message delivered in a journal article is almost always framed in a manner that promotes the author's interpretation.

It must be noted that throughout human history, no scientist has ever gotten into any serious trouble for misinterpreting results. Scientific misconduct comes, as a rule, from the purposeful production of bad data, either through falsification, fabrication, or through the refusal to remove and retract data that is known to be false, plagiarized, or otherwise invalid. In the United States, allegations of research misconduct are investigated by the The Office of Research Integrity (ORI). Funding agencies in other countries have similar watchdog institutions. The ORI makes its findings a matter of public record [18]. Of 150 cases investigated between 1993 and 1997, all but one case had an alleged component of data falsification, fabrication, or plagiarism [19]. In 2007, of the 28 investigated cases, 100% involved allegations of falsification, fabrication, or both [20]. No cases of misconduct based on data misinterpretation were prosecuted.

Postanalytic misinterpretation of data is hard-wired into the human psyche. Because data repurposing projects utilize primary data, and not the interpreted results based on the data, repurposing projects can uncover and redress misleading or erroneous results that have gained undeserved credence within the scientific community (see Glossary item, Primary data).

Case Study 5.3: The New Life Form That Wasn't: A Postanalytic Error

In 2011, amidst much fanfare, NASA scientists announced that a new form of life was found on earth, a microorganism that thrived in the high concentrations of arsenic prevalent in Mono Lake, California. The microorganism was shown to incorporate arsenic into its DNA, instead of the phosphorus used by all other known terrestrial organisms. Thus, the newfound organism synthesized a previously unencountered type of genetic material [21]. NASA's associate administrator for the Science Mission Directorate, at the time, wrote "The definition of life has just expanded" [22]. The Director of the NASA Astrobiology Institute at the agency's Ames Research Center in Moffett Field, California, wrote "Until now a life form using arsenic as a building block was only theoretical, but now we know such life exists in Mono Lake" [22].

Heady stuff! Soon thereafter, other scientists tried but failed to confirm the earlier findings [23]. It seems that the new life form was just another old life form, and the arsenic was a hard-to-wash cellular contaminant, not a fundamental constituent of the organism's genetic material.

Science is messy, even when conducted by the best of scientists and touted by the most influential and credible experts. Science operates under a burdensome rule that does not apply to religions and other belief systems: science must be validated.

5.2 UNREPEATABILITY OF COMPLEX ANALYSES

Everything has been said before, but since nobody listens we have to keep going back and beginning all over again

Andre Gide

It would seem obvious that the best way of validating research is to reproduce the research yourself. Surprisingly, this is seldom possible, particularly so in the modern research environment. Experiments may involve many different investigators, from many different institutions, using lots of expensive equipment, and producing complex datasets. Complex experiments are never easily reproduced, but simple experiments may also pose problems. The scientific literature is filled with stories of seemingly straightforward experiments that could not be repeated, either by other laboratories, or by the same laboratory on different days.

Case Study 5.4: Reality Is More Complex than We Can Ever Know

Reality is merely an illusion, albeit a very persistent one.

Albert Einstein

Andrew Nalbandov (1912–1986) was a physiologist who, in 1940, was interested in the function of the pituitary gland. The easiest way to learn something about the function of an endocrine gland involves removing it and watching what happens next. Nalbandov used chickens. When he surgically removed the pituitary, the chicken died. This was unfortunate for both the physiologist and the chicken. It is impossible to fully understand the role of the pituitary gland if removal precipitates death. Nalbandov thought that death may have resulted from poor surgical technique, so he continued conducting experiments. Sometimes the chickens survived. Sometimes they died. He could not consistently reproduce his own experiments; nor could he determine the reason for the inconsistent outcomes.

By chance one night, he noticed that the lights to his laboratory had been kept on by the janitor. After further inquiry, he found that the chickens who were kept in a lighted room postsurgery almost uniformly survived the ordeal. Quite unexpectedly, the chickens kept in darkness uniformly died. Eventually, Nalbandov discovered the physiologic basis for this phenomenon, and that is another story [24]. Finding the experimental inconsistency was a matter of luck. He had controlled the experiment as well as he could. The janitor was the wild card.

DeWitt Stetten (1909–1990) was a biochemist who, circa 1920, needed to synthesize urea from ammonium nitrate; a simple chore that would eventually open a new chapter in our understanding of biochemical physiology. Stetten used a standard, published protocol for the synthesis, but the effort did not produce the desired product (see Glossary item, Protocol). Stetten tried variations of the published protocol, unsuccessfully. Stumped, Stetten asked a colleague, Rudolf Schoenheimer, for advice. Rudolf noticed that the protocol had been published back in 1880, before glassware came into common usage in laboratories, when retorts were made of copper [24]. Stetten tried adding some copper to his substrates, and the reaction proceeded, as hoped.

We like to think that well-executed and well-documented experiments offer reproducible results. Often, they do not.

Case Study 5.5: First Biomarker Publications are Seldom Reproducible

In the past 20 years, biomarker studies have seen enormous growth: new data-intensive methodologies for biomarker development (e.g., genomics, proteomics, metabolomics), large clinical trials, much more funding support. Despite the spending surge, there has been virtually no progress in the field of biomarkers in the past several decades [14,25,26].

New biomarkers seldom achieve successful validation in other laboratories [27,26]. An article published in 2010 asserted that despite enormous efforts, only a few predictive markers have proven useful to guide breast cancer therapy; basically, molecular profiling has not been shown to have more clinical value than standard histologic methods (i.e., looking at tissues under a microscope) [28]. Not only have there been a paucity of new, validated biomarkers; the availability of large datasets has served to discredit some of the biomarkers that were previously held in high esteem [15,29].

John Ionannidis and Orestis Panagiotou reviewed published biomarker articles that had been cited in the literature more than 400 times and published in high impact journals [30]. Ionannidis and Panagiotou, along with other statisticians, have observed that the first report on a biomarker often found a larger biomarker effect size than the effect size of the same biomarker reported in subsequent studies [30,31]. Their finding is particularly disheartening considering that there is a bias that favors the perseverance of exaggerated literature claims. This reporting bias is attributed to the reluctance of authors to submit and publish findings that fail to reproduce the claims reported in earlier papers [32].

5.3 OBLIGATION TO VERIFY AND VALIDATE

Our chief want in life, is, somebody who shall make us do what we can.
Ralph Waldo Emerson, writer and philosopher (1803–1882)

There was a time when experiments were cheap, easy, and quick. You didn't need to take anyone's word for the results. You could repeat the experiment for yourself. As previously noted, modern experiments are complex and cannot be repeated. The best we can do is to verify and validate these studies.

There are three common terms that are defined somewhat differently by data scientists, leading to considerable confusion: Reproducibility, Validation, and Verification. The definitions that follow are unlikely to be adopted uniformly within the field of data science, but at the very least, they may help readers appreciate the discussion that follows.

Reproducibility is achieved when the repitition of a study produces the same data (i.e., results) over and over. Reproducibility is closely related to validation, which is achieved when you draw the same conclusions, from the data, over and over again [33]. Verification is the process by which data is checked to determine that it was obtained properly (i.e., according to approved protocols), and that the data measures what it was intended to measure, on the correct specimens.

For example, a massive or complex data resource might contain position, velocity, direction, and mass data for the earth and for a meteor that is traveling sunwards. The data meets all specifications for measurement, error tolerance, data typing, and data completeness; hence, the data is verified. Repeating the measurements produces the same results; hence, the data is reproducible. An analysis of the data indicates that the meteor will miss the earth by a safe 50,000 miles, plus or minus 10,000 miles. If the asteroid smashes into the earth, destroying all planetary life, then an extraterrestrial observer might conclude that the data was verified and reproducible, but not validated.

In a 2012 publication, the U.S. National Academy of Sciences tackled the vexing problem of data validation in a book entitled "Assessing the Reliability of Complex Models: Mathematical and Statistical Foundations of Verification, Validation, and Uncertainty Quantification" [33]. Not surprisingly, the authors found that there are many different ways of analyzing the same data, and these ways often included parametric and nonparametric techniques, computer models, approximations achieved without a computer model, exact models, and neural networks (see Glossary items, Neural network, Nonparametric statistics). Furthermore, with access to large complex datasets, scientists can now rummage through the data, finding statistically significant effects, that are not validated by any reproducibly measurable biological effect (see Glossary item, Multiple comparison bias) [31]. This being the case, it is imperative that all analyses should be validated to show that comparable conclusions are obtained whenever suitable analytic methods are employed. Furthermore, validation requires access to the same data that was available to the scientists who published the original set of conclusions, and to additional datasets that provide external confirmation of the original conclusions.

Case Study 5.6: Reanalysis Clarifies Earlier Findings

Harold Gatty gained fame, in 1931, when he navigated an 8-day flight around the world. During World War II, he taught navigation and directed Air Transport for the allies in the Pacific campaign. His most enduring legacy has been his book "Finding Your Way Without Map or Compass" in which he explains how to determine your location and direction, the time of day, and, the season of the year, the day of the month, and the approaching weather, from simple observations [34]. Gatty cautioned against overconfidence, insisting that navigators should never depend on a single observation "as it may be an exception to the general rule. It is the combined evidence of a number of different indications which strengthens and confirms the conclusions" [34].

Gatty's comment on the significance of observations in the natural world applies to statistical analyses in general. Monsanto, a large agricultural company, seeking regulatory approval for its new, genetically modified corn, conducted a 90-day toxicity trial. A review of the results led to the conclusion that the corn was nontoxic. A second analysis of the same results led to another conclusion entirely; that the study showed evidence of liver and kidney toxicity.

What do you do when two analyses of the same results produce two different conclusions? One option is to repeat the study. Another option is to call in an expert panel to review the two analyses and to render an opinion as to which analysis is correct. The latter option is sometimes preferable if the first study seems to have been conducted properly, or if the study would be difficult to repeat.

In this case, an expert panel was convened [35]. The panel concluded that the liver and kidney toxicity reported in the second analysis of the data had statistical reproducibility (i.e., the results could be faithfully recomputed from the data), but that the findings lacked biological significance. The panel looked for, but failed to find, any relationship between the size of the dose and the level of toxicity. Furthermore, there seemed to be no relationship between the length of exposure time and subsequent toxicity. In addition, there were no morphologic alterations found in the livers and kidneys of affected animals that would indicate a toxic effect. The findings were not consistent with the kinds of biological effects that would be expected from a toxin. In this example, the Expert Panel refused to draw a conclusion based on one statistically abnormal measurement. In essence, the Expert Panel followed Gatty's advice and looked for additional signs that they would expect to find if the statistical conclusions were true [35].

There is no statute of limitations on data reanalysis.

Case Study 5.7: It Is Never Too Late to Review Old Data

John Seabrook chronicled the efforts of ornithologist Pamela Rasmussen (born 1959), who uncovered a fraud, committed throughout the first half of the twentieth century, involving numerous bird specimens collected through the latter half of the nineteenth century [36]. The culprit was Colonel Richard Meinertzhagen (1878–1967). He stole bird specimens from historical collections and annotated them with fabricated data. The scientific mischief came to light in the early 1990s by Pamela Rasmussen and Robert Prys-Jones, who found inconsistencies in curated bird specimens. There were bird species reported to come from areas where the bird species did not exist, and there were bird specimens containing samples consistent with collections that predated Meinertzhagen, prepared with techniques that were different from those employed by Meinertzhagen. After the investigation, dozens of taxa had to be removed from the British list. Throughout Meinertzhagen's long life, his many scientific fabrications went undiscovered.

Although there are occasions when reanalysis will discredit published conclusions, it should not be forgotten that the most important role of reanalysis is to confirm, strengthen, and extend prior knowledge.

Case Study 5.8: Vindication Through Reanalysis

In 1978, Joseph Strauch published a phylogenetic taxonomy of Charadriiformes birds (i.e., a subclassification based on evolutionary descent), by studying their bones (i.e., via osteology) [37]. When he finished his project, he left his osteologic data for others to reanalyze. As it happened, his conclusions stirred a controversy that persisted over several decades. Nearly 20 years later, Phillip Chu took a hard look at Strauch's measurements [38]. Chu recoded Strauch's data to eliminate objectionable feature assignments. Chu conducted a parsimony analysis of the data rather than using Strauch's compatibility analysis; both being methods that establish phylogenetic order. In the end, Chu's study confirmed Strauch's findings.

It is not easy to publish journal manuscripts that vindicate earlier works. Journal editors, traditionally, are interested in publishing new science; not in revisiting previously published studies. It is plausible that Chu's paper, reanalyzing Strauch's work, was worthy of publication only because Strauch's early work had been publicly challenged [39]. Journal editors should be receptive to reanalysis manuscripts as they often provide new insights that advance their fields [40]. In addition, there are occasions when reanalysis is the only method by which scientific truth can be established.

Reanalysis can only be performed on studies for which data is available. Scientists can avoid having their studies reanalyzed by simply withholding their data from their colleagues.

Case Study 5.9: Reanalysis Bias

In 2011, Jelte Wicherts and colleagues conducted a study in which they looked at papers that were reanalyzed by others. They found that researchers that had very good data, supporting unambiguous conclusions, were, generally, willing to share their data. Researchers who had weak data, that might support various interpretations and contrasting conclusions, were less willing to share their data [41].

Based on this study, which itself needs to be repeated and reanalyzed, there is a systemic bias in scientific reanalysis. Reanalysis is most often performed on studies with high quality data and strong conclusions; the studies in least need of reanalysis. Studies based on weak data that produce arguable conclusions are seldom reanalyzed; these being the studies in greatest need of reanalysis.

5.4 ASKING WHAT THE DATA REALLY MEANS

The question is not what you look at, but what you see.
Henry David Thoreau in his journal, August 5, 1851

Every dataset has a story to tell, and the story often unfolds in ways that were not anticipated by the people who collected the data.

Case Study 5.10: Repurposing the Logarithmic Tables

In 1614, John Napier (1550–1617), a Scottish mathematician, published tables of logarithms and antilogarithms. The primary purpose of these tables was to facilitate multiplication, division, and exponentiation. The mathematical formula that was the basis of logarithmic operations is as follows:

if $a = b \times c$
then $\log(a) = \log(b \times c) = \log(b) + \log(c)$
and $\operatorname{antilog}(\log(a)) = \operatorname{antilog}(\log(b) + \log(c))$
or $a = \operatorname{antilog}((\log(b)) + (\log(c)))$

Simply put, you can multiply together any collection of numbers by summing all of their logarithmic values and then taking the antilog of the sum. Division works much the same way, but the logarithms of the divisors are subtracted from the sum.

Anyone who owned a copy of Napier's logarithmic and antilogarithmic tables could perform hitherto tedious computations with ease. It seems implausible nowadays, but former generations of students practiced their multiplications and divisions, using published logarithmic tables, until such time that they attained speed and proficiency at the task.

Eight years following the Napier's publication of the logarithmic tables, some clever person repurposed the tables by marking them upon wooden rulers designed to slide over one another. In this manner, consecutive multiplication operations could be accomplished by aligning the rulers over the logarithm values of number to be multiplied together, thus reaching the summed logarithm and its marked antilogarithm (i.e., the answer to the multiplication). Anyone handy with a slide rule could multiply and divide a succession of numbers, with great ease and with passable accuracy. Elaborate slide rules were constructed for more advanced mathematical operations. Go back in time and ask any engineer, working between 1650 and 1950; they will tell you that no calculating device will ever replace their trusted slide rule.

The slide rule, popular for nearly 350 years, was eventually replaced by the electronic calculator. Needless to say, the slide rule could not have been invented before the table of logarithmic numbers was made available. The invention of the slide rule was one of the earliest and most enduring triumphs of data repurposing.

Case Study 5.11: Multimodality in Legacy Data

Multimodal data distributions have more than one peak. Multimodality always tells us something very important about the data distribution. For example, Hodgkin lymphoma, an uncommon type of human cancer, has a well-known bimodal age distribution (Figure 5.1). Examination of a large dataset collected on individuals with Hodgkin lymphoma indicates that there is a peak in occurrences at a young age and another peak of occurrences at a more advanced age [42].

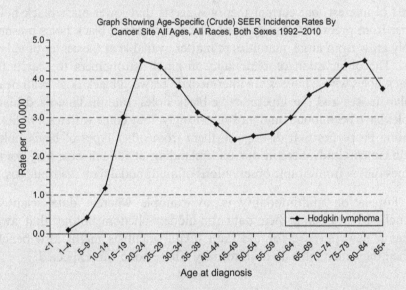

Figure 5.1 The number of occurrences of Hodgkin Lymphoma in persons of different ages. There are two peaks, one at about 35 years of age and another peak at about 75 years of age. The distribution appears to be bimodal [43]. The National Cancer Institute's Surveillance Epidemiology End Results, public domain [44].

In the case of Hodgkin lymphoma, lymphomas occurring in the young may share diagnostic features with the lymphomas occurring in an older population, but the occurrence of lymphomas in two separable populations may indicate that some important distinction was overlooked: a different etiology (i.e., cause) for tumors occurring in the two age categories, or different genetic alterations in the two age sets, or two different types of lymphomas that were mistakenly classified under one name, or two separable genetic populations [45], or some flaw in the data (e.g., misdiagnoses, mix-ups during data collection). Explaining the causes for data incongruities is always a scientific challenge. At the current time, the appearance of a bimodal age distribution for Hodgkin lymphoma is a curiosity of medicine.

The importance of inspecting data for multimodality also applies to black holes. Most black holes have mass equivalents under 33 solar masses. Another set of black holes are supermassive with mass equivalents of 10 or 20 billion solar masses. When there are objects of the same type, whose masses differ by a factor of a billion, scientists infer that there is something fundamentally different in the origin or development of these two variant forms of the same object. Black hole formation is an active area of interest, but current theory suggests that lower mass black holes arise from preexisting heavy stars. The supermassive black holes presumably grow from large quantities of matter available at the center of galaxies. The observation of bimodality inspired astronomers to search for black holes whose masses are intermediate between black holes with near-solar masses and the supermassive black holes. Intermediate-sized black holes have been found, and, not surprisingly, they come with a set of fascinating properties that distinguish them from other types of black holes. Fundamental advances in our understanding of the universe may sometimes follow from simple observations of multimodal data distributions.

Population multimodality is an example wherein data scientists benefit by searching their data for hidden phenomenology that awakens a new purpose for old data. Data scientists might also benefit when they encounter data uniformity where none was expected.

Case Study 5.12: The Significance of Narrow Data Ranges

Anyone interested in analyzing the earliest hospital-acquired legacy data must go back to 1868, when Carl Wunderlich published Das Verhalten der Eigenwarme in Krankheiten, his collection of body temperature data on approximately 25,000 patients [46]. Wunderlich's work sparked considerable debate over the best way of visualizing large datasets. Competing suggestions for the representation of thermometric data, as it was called, included time interval (i.e., discontinuous) graphs and oscillating real-time (i.e., continuous) temperature charts. Soon thereafter, the practice of collecting blood pressure data became common practice. Standard bedside recordings of pulse, blood pressure, respirations, and temperature eventually came to be known as "vital signs."

As bedside measurements became commonplace, a variety of blood tests were developed. By the third decade of the twentieth century, physicians had at their disposal most of the common blood tests known to modern medicine (e.g., electrolytes, blood cells, lipids, glucose, nitrogenous compounds).

What the early twentieth century physicians lacked was any sensible way to interpret the test results. Learning how to interpret blood tests required examination of old data on many thousands of individuals, and it took considerable time and effort to interpret the aggregated results.

The most remarkable, and enduring, finding from these early studies was that blood tests performed on normal populations produced results that fell into a very narrow range. This was particularly true for electrolytes (e.g., sodium and calcium) and to a somewhat lesser extent for blood cells (e.g., white blood cells, red blood cells). Furthermore, for any individual, multiple recordings at different times of the day and on different days tended to produce consistent results (e.g., sodium concentration in the morning was equivalent to sodium concentration in the evening). These findings were totally unexpected, at the time.

Analysis of the data also showed that significant deviations from the normal concentrations of any one of these blood chemicals are always an indicator of disease. Backed by data, but lacking any deep understanding of the physiologic role of blood components, physicians learned to associate abnormal blood test results with specific diseases.

The observation of a narrow normal range, in a variety of blood tests, and the association of deviations from the normal range with specific disease processes, was the most important breakthrough in medicine in the first two decades of the twentieth century. The discovery of the "normal range" revolutionized the field of physiology. Thereafter, physiologists concentrated their efforts toward understanding how the body regulates its blood constituents. Their early studies led to nearly everything we now know about homeostatic control mechanisms.

REFERENCES

[1] Unreliable research: trouble at the lab. The Economist, October 19, 2013.

[2] Prasad V, Vandross A, Toomey C, Cheung M, Rho J, Quinn S, et al. A decade of reversal: an analysis of 146 contradicted medical practices. Mayo Clin Proc 2013;88:790−8.

[3] Kolata G. Cancer fight: unclear tests for new drug. The New York Times; April 19, 2010.

[4] Ioannidis JP. Why most published research findings are false. PLoS Med 2005;2:e124.

[5] Knight J. Agony for researchers as mix-up forces retraction of ecstasy study. Nature 2003;425:109.

[6] Andrew SE, Goldberg YP, Kremer B, Squitieri F, Theilmann J, Zeisler J, et al. Huntington disease without CAG expansion: phenocopies or errors in assignment? Am J Hum Genet 1994;54:852–63.

[7] Bandelt H, Salas A. Contamination and sample mix-up can best explain some patterns of mtDNA instabilities in buccal cells and oral squamous cell carcinoma. BMC Cancer 2009;9:113.

[8] Palanichamy MG, Zhang Y. Potential pitfalls in MitoChip detected tumor-specific somatic mutations: a call for caution when interpreting patient data. BMC Cancer 2010;10:597.

[9] Sainani K. Error: what biomedical computing can learn from its mistakes. Biomed Comput Rev 2011;12–19.

[10] Satter RG. UK investigates 800,000 organ donor list errors. Associated Press; April 10, 2010.

[11] Robertson P, Mahadevan S, Endl M, Roy A. Exoplanet detection. Stellar activity masquerading as planets in the habitable zone of the M dwarf Gliese 581. Science 2014;345:440–4.

[12] Ioannidis JP. Is molecular profiling ready for use in clinical decision making? Oncologist 2007;12:301–11.

[13] Ioannidis JP. Some main problems eroding the credibility and relevance of randomized trials. Bull NYU Hosp Jt Dis 2008;66:135–9.

[14] Ioannidis JP. Microarrays and molecular research: noise discovery? Lancet 2005;365:454–5.

[15] Ioannidis JP, Panagiotou OA. Comparison of effect sizes associated with biomarkers reported in highly cited individual articles and in subsequent meta-analyses. JAMA 2011;305:2200–10.

[16] Berman JJ. Principles of big data: preparing, sharing, and analyzing complex information. Burlington, MA: Morgan Kaufmann; 2013.

[17] Wilson JR. Rhetorical strategies used in the reporting of implantable defibrillator primary prevention trials. Am J Cardiol 2011;107:1806–11.

[18] Office of Research Integrity. Available from: <http://ori.dhhs.gov>.

[19] Scientific Misconduct Investigations. 1993–1997. Office of Research Integrity, Office of Public Health and Science, Department of Health and Human Services, December 1998.

[20] Office of Research Integrity Annual Report 2007, June 2008. Available from: <http://ori.hhs.gov/images/ddblock/ori_annual_report_2007.pdf> [01.01.15].

[21] Wolfe-Simon F, Switzer Blum J, Kulp TR, Gordon GW, Hoeft SE, Pett-Ridge J, et al. A bacterium that can grow by using arsenic instead of phosphorus. Science 2011;332:1163–6.

[22] Discovery of "Arsenic-bug" expands definition of life. NASA, December 2, 2010.

[23] Reaves ML, Sinha S, Rabinowitz JD, Kruglyak L, Redfield RJ. Absence of arsenate in DNA from arsenate-grown GFAJ-1 cells. Science 2012;337:470–3.

[24] Gratzer W. Eurekas and euphorias: The Oxford book of scientific anecdotes. Oxford, United Kingdom: Oxford University Press; 2002.

[25] Benowitz S. Biomarker boom slowed by validation concerns. J Natl Cancer Inst 2004;96:1356–7.

[26] Abu-Asab MS, Chaouchi M, Alesci S, Galli S, Laassri M, Cheema AK, et al. Biomarkers in the age of omics: time for a systems biology approach. OMICS 2011;15:105–12.

[27] Begley S. In cancer science, many "discoveries" don't hold up. Reuters March 28, 2012.

[28] Weigelt B, Reis-Filho JS. Molecular profiling currently offers no more than tumour morphology and basic immunohistochemistry. Breast Cancer Res 2010;12:S5.

[29] Moyer VA, on behalf of the U.S. Preventive Services Task Force. Screening for prostate cancer: U.S. Preventive Services Task Force recommendation statement. Ann Intern Med 2011.

[30] Ioannidis JPA, Panagiotou OA. Comparison of effect sizes associated with biomarkers reported in highly cited individual articles and in subsequent meta-analyses. JAMA 2011;305:2200–10.

[31] Nuzzo R. P values, the gold standard of statistical validity, are not as reliable as many scientists assume. Nature 2014;506:150–2.

[32] Ioannidis JP. Excess significance bias in the literature on brain volume abnormalities. Arch Gen Psychiatry 2011;68:773–80.

[33] Committee on Mathematical Foundations of Verification, Validation, and Uncertainty Quantification; Board on Mathematical Sciences and Their Applications, Division on Engineering and Physical Sciences, National Research Council. Assessing the reliability of complex models: mathematical and statistical foundations of verification, validation, and uncertainty quantification. National Academy Press, 2012. Available from: <http://www.nap.edu/catalog.php?record_id = 13395> [accessed 01.01.15].

[34] Gatty H. Finding your way without map or compass. Mineola, NY: Dover; 1958.

[35] Doull J, Gaylor D, Greim HA, Lovell DP, Lynch B, Munro IC. Report of an expert panel on the reanalysis by of a 90-day study conducted by Monsanto in support of the safety of a genetically modified corn variety (MON 863). Food Chem Toxicol 2007;45:2073–85.

[36] Seabrook J. Ruffled feathers. The New Yorker; May 29, 2006.

[37] Strauch JG. The phylogeny of the Charadriiformes (Aves): a new estimate using the method of character compatibility analysis. Trans Zool Soc Lond 1978;34:263–345.

[38] Chu PC. Phylogenetic reanalysis of Strauch's osteological data set for the Charadriiformes. Condor 1995;97:174–96.

[39] Mickevich MF, Parenti LR. Review of "The phylogeny of the Charadriiformes (Aves):a new estimate using the method of character compatibility analysis." Syst Zool 1980;29:108–13.

[40] Bochdanovits Z, Verhage M, Smit AB, de Geus EJ, Posthuma D, Boomsma DI, et al. Joint reanalysis of 29 correlated SNPs supports the role of PCLO/Piccolo as a causal risk factor for major depressive disorder. Mol Psychiatry 2009;14:650–2.

[41] Wicherts JM, Bakker M, Molenaar D. Willingness to share research data is related to the strength of the evidence and the quality of reporting of statistical results. PLoS One 2011;6(11):e26828.

[42] Berman JJ. Methods in medical informatics: fundamentals of healthcare programming in Perl, Python, and Ruby. Boca Raton, FL: Chapman and Hall; 2010.

[43] Berman JJ. Rare diseases and orphan drugs: keys to understanding and treating common diseases. Waltham, MA: Academic Press; 2014.

[44] SEER. Surveillance Epidemiology End Results. National Cancer Institute. Available from: <http://seer.cancer.gov/>.

[45] Grotmol T, Bray F, Holte H, Haugen M, Kunz L, Tretli S, et al. Frailty modeling of the bimodal age-incidence of Hodgkin lymphoma in the Nordic countries. Cancer Epidemiol Biomarkers Prev 2011;20:1350–7.

[46] Wunderlich CR. Das Verhalten der Eigenw rme in Krankheiten ("The behavior of the self-warmth in diseases"). Leipzig: O. Wigand; 1868.

CHAPTER 6

Dark Legacy: Making Sense of Someone Else's Data

6.1 EXCAVATING TREASURES FROM LOST AND ABANDONED DATA MINES

"We've got no money, so we've got to think."—Ernest Rutherford, who, as director of the Cavendish Laboratory at Cambridge University, supported Nobel prize winning researchers, with minimal funding

Data mining is closely related to data repurposing, but there is one key difference. Data miners use data for its intended purposes. Hence, the data that they use is, more often than not, prepared in a format that facilitates analysis. Data repurposers use data for purposes that were unintended or unimagined by the people who prepared the data. Hence, data repurposers, more often than not, must locate, unearth, resurrect, revitalize, and transform the data into something worth analyzing.

Case Study 6.1: Reanalysis of Old JADE Collider Data

In the 1980s, the PETRA collider conducted a number of so-called atom smashing experiments designed to measure the force required to bind together quarks and gluons, the fundamental components of protons and neutrons. In 1986, the PETRA collider was decommissioned and replaced with colliders that operated at higher energy levels. Several decades past and advances in physics raised questions that could only be answered with observations on low-energy collisions; the kind of observations collected by PETRA and omitted by present-day colliders [1].

An effort to retrieve and repurpose the 1980s data was spearheaded by Siegfried Bethke, one of the original scientists in PETRA's JADE project [2]. In the period following the decommissioning of PETRA, the original data had been dispersed to various laboratories. Some of the JADE data was simply lost, and none of the data was collected in a format or a medium that was directly accessible.

The repurposing project was divided into three tasks, involving three teams of scientists. One team rescued the data for archived tapes and transferred the data into a modern medium and format. The second team improved the original JADE software, fitting it to modern computer platforms. By applying new software, using updated Monte Carlo simulations, the second team generated a new set of data files (see Glossary item, Monte Carlo simulation). The third team reanalyzed the regenerated data using modern methods and improved calculations.

The project culminated in the production of numerous scientific contributions that could not have been achieved without the old JADE data. Success was credited, at least in part, to the participation of some of the same individuals who collected the original data.

Because data repurposing often involves data that large federal or private agencies have abandoned, such projects may attract resourceful data scavengers.

Case Study 6.2: 36-Year-Old Satellite Resurrected

The International Space/Earth Explorer 3 (ISEE-3) spacecraft was launched in 1978 and proceeded on a successful mission to monitor the interaction between the solar wind and the earth's magnetic field.

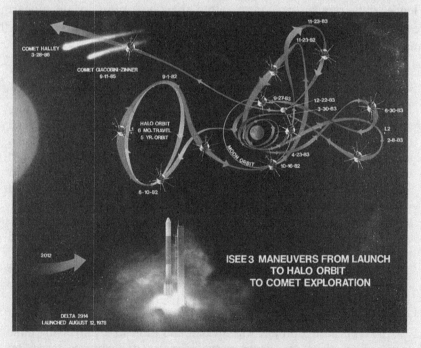

Figure 6.1 Trajectory of the International Cometary Explorer. NASA, public domain.

In 1985, ISEE-3 visited the comet Giacobini-Zinner and was thereupon given a new name, ICE (the International Cometary Explorer). In 1999 NASA, short of funds, decommissioned ICE. In 2008, NASA tried to contact ICE and found that all but one of its 13 observational experiments were still in operation, and that the spacecraft had not yet exhausted its propellant (Figure 6.1).

In April 2014, a citizens group of interested scientists and engineers announced their intention to reboot ICE [3]. In May 2014, NASA entered into a Non-Reimbursable Space Act Agreement with the citizens group, which would provide the reboot team with NASA advisors, but no funding. Later in May, the team successfully commanded the probe to broadcast its telemetry (i.e., its recorded data). In September, the team lost contact with ICE. ICE will return to a near-earth position, in 17 years. There is reason to hope that scientists will eventually recover ICE telemetry, and, with it, find new opportunities for data repurposing.

6.2 NONSTANDARD STANDARDS

The nice thing about standards is that you have so many to choose from.
Andrew S. Tanenbaum

Standards are the false gods of informatics. Like so many gods that have come and gone, each demanded that their followers obey their laws and accept no other gods. In exchange, they promised eternal life and harmony. Instead, they delivered chaos and destruction.

The major problem with standards is that they change all the time. In many cases, as a standard matures, it becomes hopelessly complex. As the complexity becomes unmanageable, those who profess to use the standard may develop their own idiosyncratic implementations. Organizations that produce standards seldom provide a mechanism to ensure that the standard is implemented correctly. Standards have long been plagued by noncompliance or (more frequently) under-compliance. Over time, so-called standard-compliant systems tend to become incompatible with one another. The net result is that legacy data, purported to conform to a standard format, is no longer understandable.

If you take the time to read some of the computer literature from the 1970s or 1980s, you will come across the names of standards that have long-since fallen into well-deserved obscurity. You may find that the literature from the 1970s is nearly impossible to read with any level of comprehension, due to the large number of now-obsolete acronyms scattered through every page. **Today's eternal standard is tomorrow's indecipherable gibberish.**

The Open Systems Interconnection (OSI) was an internet protocol created in 1977 with approval from the International Organization for Standardization. It has been supplanted by TCP/IP, the protocol that everyone uses today. A handful of programming languages have been recognized as standards by the American National Standards Institute. These include Basic, C, Ada, and Mumps. Basic and C are still popular languages. Ada, recommended by the Federal Government, back in 1995, as the recommended language for all high performance software applications, is virtually forgotten [4]. Mumps is still in use, particularly in hospital information systems, but it changed its name to M, lost its allure to a new generation of programmers, and now comes in various implementations that may not strictly conform to the original standard.

Despite the problems inherent in standards, government committees cling to standards as the best way to share data. Here is an excerpt from a report issued by the Committee on Vital Health Statistics issued in 2000. "Without national standard vocabularies, precise clinical data collection and accurate interpretation of such data is difficult to achieve. Further, this lack of standard vocabularies makes it difficult to study best practices and develop clinical decision support" [5].

Raymond Kammer, then Director of the U.S. National Institute of Standards and Technology, understood the downside of standards. In a year 2000 government report, he wrote that "the consequences of standards can be negative. For example, companies and nations can use standards to disadvantage competitors. Embodied in national regulations, standards can be crafted to impede export access, sometimes necessitating excessive testing and even redesigns of products. A 1999 survey by the National Association of Manufacturers reported that about half of US small manufacturers find international standards or product certification requirements to be barriers to trade. And according to the Transatlantic Business Dialogue, differing requirements add more than 10% to the cost of car design and development" [6].

As we shall discuss again, when we cover ontologies later in this chapter (Section 6.4), standard representations of data and of concepts are difficult to achieve.

Case Study 6.3: Standardizing the Chocolate Teapot [7]

Malcolm Duncan has posted an insightful and funny essay entitled "The Chocolate Teapot (Version 2.3)" [8]. In this essay, he shows how new versions of nomenclatures may unintentionally alter the meanings of terms contained in earlier versions, making it impossible to compare or sensibly aggregate terms and concepts contained in any of the versions.

Suppose you have a cooking-ware terminology with a "teapot" item. Version one of the nomenclature may list only one teapot material, porcelain, and only two permissible teapot colors, blue or white. Version 2 of the terminology might accommodate the two teapot subtypes: blue teapot and white teapot (i.e., in version 2, blue and white are subtypes of teapot, not colors of teapot). If a teapot was neither blue nor white, it would be coded under the parent term "teapot." Suppose version 3 accommodates some new additions to the teapot pantheon: chocolate teapot, ornamental teapot, china teapot, and industrial teapot. Now the teapot world is shaken by a tempest of monumental proportions. The white and blue teapots had been implicitly considered to be made of porcelain, like all china teapots. How does one deal with a white teapot that is not porcelain or a porcelain teapot that is not a china teapot? If we had previously assumed that a teapot was an item in which tea is made, how do we adjust, conceptually, to the new term "ornamental teapot?" If the teapot is ornamental, then it has no tea-making functionality, and if it cannot be used to make tea, how can it be a teapot? Must we change our concept of the teapot to mean anything that looks like a teapot? If so, how can we deal with the new term "industrial teapot," which is likely to be a big stainless steel vat that has more in common, structurally, with a microbrewery fermenter than with an ornamental teapot? What is the meaning of a chocolate teapot? Is it something made of chocolate, is it chocolate-colored, or does it brew chocolate-flavored tea? Suddenly we have lost the ability to map terms in version 3 to terms in versions 1 and 2. We no longer understand the classes of objects (i.e., teapots) in the various versions of our cookware nomenclature. We cannot unambiguously attach nomenclature terms to objects in our data collection (e.g., blue china teapot). We no longer have a precise definition of a teapot or of the subtypes of teapot.

Regarding versioning, it is a very good rule of thumb that when you encounter a standard whose name includes a version number (e.g., International Classification of Diseases-10, Diagnostic and Statistical Manual of Mental Disorders-5), you can be certain that the standard is unstable, and must be continually revised. Some standards survive, when they really deserve to die. In some cases, a poor standard is kept alive indefinitely by influential leaders in their fields, or by entities who have an economic stake in perpetuating the standard.

Data managers are often unaware of the many standards to which they must comply. If they were presented, early in their careers, with the body of standards that they would need to learn, and if they understood that all of these standards would be growing more complex, over time, and that there would be new standards to replace these old standards, and that layers of standardization would be added to their burden, then there might be a mass exodus of data managers as they poured into less standardized occupations (e.g., authoring textbooks).

6.3 SPECIFICATIONS, NOT STANDARDS

Good specifications will always improve programmer productivity far better than any programming tool or technique.

Milt Bryce

Although informaticians often use the terms "specification" and "standard" interchangeably, the two terms are quite different from one another. A specification is a formal way of describing data. A standard is a set of requirements, created by a standards development organization, that comprise a predetermined content and format for a set of data.

Specifications, unlike standards, do not tell you what data must be included in a document, or how that data must be formatted within the document. A specification simply provides a uniform way of representing the information you choose to include, and it provides suggestions for the kinds of information that would help others understand what the document is trying to say, and how it can be used.

For example, there is a set of basic self-identifying information that every electronic file or document would benefit by including. These include such information as the date that the file was created, the name of the entity that created the file, the name of the owner of the file, any restrictions on the public use of the file (e.g., a copyright statement), a general comment on the contents of the file, and a location where the metadata used within the file is defined, if it is not defined within the file (see Glossary item, ISO 11179). The specification for general file descriptors is the Dublin Core. These data elements, developed by a committee of librarians, specify the header information in electronic files and documents. The syntax for the Dublin Core specification is found at: http://dublincore.org/documents/dces/.

Following the preliminary self-descriptive file header comes the file's data. Each data element is annotated with metadata, the data that describes data. For example, a data element may consist of the number "150." The metadata for the data may be the words "Weight, in pounds." The syntax for listing a metadata/data pair might consist of bracketed metadata enclosing the data element and would look something like the following:

```
<weight_in_pounds>150</weight_in_pounds>.
```

A data point is useless without its metadata, and metadata is useless if it does not convey the information that adequately describes the data element. Metadata annotations help us relate data objects that reside in diverse datasets. Imagine that you have spent the past decade building an annotated database named "Postage Stamps of the World." Your friends tease you mercilessly, believing that you have wasted your time on philately. What might you say to defend your passion? You might explain that your well-annotated postage stamp ontology is integrated into other databases covering geographic regions, economies, populations, and cultures. By graphing the price of stamps, country-by-country, you can determine which countries must have endured times of hyperinflation, reflected as huge rises in the cost of postage. By matching the human faces featured on stamps, by country, you can determine which cultures value scientific achievement (e.g., by featuring Nobel laureates), which countries value entertainment (e.g., by featuring musicians), and which countries value armed conflict (e.g., by featuring generals and war heroes). You can link countries to various political and social persuasions by studying the slogans that appear on stamps (e.g., calls to war, pleas for conservation, faith-based icons). Animals featured on stamps tell you something about local fauna. Examining the production levels of postage stamps within a country (i.e., the number of postage stamps printed per capita), you gather that certain countries have been using postage stamps as legal tender, in lieu of minted bills. If stamps from multiple countries have the same basic design, then you can infer that these countries are too small to design and print their own stamps, and have opted to use the same manufacturer. In all of these cases, the well-annotated stamp is a window to the world, providing an unbiased and hyperconnected view of reality. The friends who teased you did not understand that data can be repurposed if it is well-annotated. In the world of data repurposing, the value of data has less to do with the subject matter of the data, and more to do with the quality of annotation and the linkages to other datasets.

A specification serves most of the purposes of a standard, plus providing many important functionalities that standards typically lack (e.g., full data description, data exchange across diverse types of datasets, data merging, and semantic logic). Data specifications spare us most of the heavy baggage that comes with standards, which includes: limited flexibility to include changing data objects, locked-in data descriptors, licensing and other intellectual property issues, competition among standards that compete within the same data domain, and bureaucratic overhead (see Glossary item, Intellectual property).

Case Study 6.4: The Fungibility of Data Standards

Data standards, like all other electronic objects, are collections of 0 s and 1 s. Hence, you can convert one standard into another standard and one version of a standard into another version of the same standard; if you try hard enough.

For example, there are dozens of image formats (e.g., jpeg, png, gif, tiff). Although these formats have not gone through a standards development process, they are used by millions of individuals and have achieved the status as *de facto* standards. For most of us, the selection of any image format is not crucial. We all have access to robust image software that will convert images from one format to another. For example, ImageMagick is a no cost, widely available, open-source software that can create, edit, compose, or convert images (see Glossary items, Open access, Open source). After ImageMagick is installed, we can convert between image formats from the command line:

```
c:\ >convert cloud.jpg cloud.png
```

Likewise, there are methods available that permit us to add specifying information to the image headers for any image file, stored in any image format [9].

Basically, files constructed in any chosen data standard can be converted to and from any other data standard that encapsulates the same kinds of information contained in the original standard, or to any specification that defines metadata for a standard's data elements.

The most common mistake committed by data scientists is to convert legacy data directly into a contemporary standard, and using analytic software that is designed to operate exclusively upon the chosen standard. Doing so only serves to perpetuate legacy-related frustrations. You can be certain that your data standard and your software application will be unsuitable for the next generation of data scientists. It makes much more sense to port legacy data into a general specification, from which data can be ported to any current or future data standard.

6.4 CLASSIFICATIONS AND ONTOLOGIES

The ignoramus is a leaf who doesn't know he is part of a tree
attributed to Michael Crichton

The human brain is constantly processing visual and other sensory information collected from the environment. When we walk down the street, we see images of concrete and asphalt and grass and persons and birds and so on. Every step we take conveys another world of sensory input. How can we process it all? The mathematician and philosopher Karl Pearson (1857–1936) has likened the human mind to a "sorting machine" [10]. We take a stream of sensory information and sort it into objects, and then we collect the individual objects into general classes. The green stuff on the ground is classified as "grass," and the grass is subclassified under some larger group such as "plants." Flat stretches of asphalt and concrete may be classified under "road" and the road might be subclassified under "man-made constructions." If we did not have a culturally determined classification of objects in the world, we would have no languages, no ability to communicate ideas, no way to remember what we see, and no way to draw general inferences about anything at all. Simply put, without classifications, we would not be able to think, and we would not be human [11].

Every culture has some particular way to impose a uniform way of perceiving the environment. In English-speaking cultures, the term "hat" denotes a universally recognized object. Hats may be composed of many different types of materials, and they may vary greatly in size, weight, and shape. Nonetheless, we can almost always identify a hat when we see one, and we can distinguish a hat from all other types of objects. An object is not classified as a hat simply because it shares a few structural similarities with other hats. A hat is classified as a hat because it has a relationship to every other hat, as an item of clothing that fits over the head. Likewise, all classifications are built by relationships, not by similarities [11,12].

In Section 2.5, we defined classifications as systems in which every object instance in a knowledge domain is assigned to a class within a linear hierarchy of classes (see Glossary item, Instance). In a classification, every class has one immediate superclass. The immediate superclass of a class is called the parent class. The immediate subclass of a class is called the child class (see Glossary items, Parent class, Child class).

Ontologies are classifications in which a class can have more than one immediate superclass (see Glossary item, Ontology). Classifications can be thought of as the simplest and most restrictive type of ontology. The advantage of a classification, over a multiparental ontology, is that classifications are easier to understand, and they drive down the complexity of their knowledge domain [13]. In addition, classifications can be easily modeled in an object-oriented programming language and are nonchaotic (i.e., calculations performed on the members and classes of a classification should yield the same output, each time the calculation is performed). The advantage of ontologies is that they model classes of objects that logically have more than one superclass (e.g., a human can be an animal and an insurance agent), and an ontology can be constructed as a rule-based system in which members of classes obey all of the rules that apply to all of their parental and ancestral classes.

For the data scientist, every class, within a classification or an ontology, is a key that connects the members of the class to the members of related classes. Despite the importance of classifications, few data scientists receive much training on the subject. It is often assumed, incorrectly, that everyone knows how to sensibly organize their own data. Actually, the design of classifications and ontologies is difficult and is often done incorrectly.

Ontologists understand that specialized ontologies must fit somewhere within more generalized ontologies, that encompass everything in our universe. If I am preparing an ontology of stamps, I know in advance that each stamp is issued by a specific country, and I will want to link the stamp, in my stamp ontology, to a country name that belongs to an ontology of geopolitical entities. An ontology of geopolitical entities should indicate that its members belong to earth, and the object known as earth should link to a higher ontology that includes classes of planets.

Case Study 6.5: An Upper Level Ontology

Knowing that ontologies reach into higher ontologies, ontologists have endeavored to create upper level ontologies to accommodate general classes of objects, under which the lower ontologies may take their place.

One such ontology is SUMO, the Suggested Upper Merged Ontology, created by a group of talented ontologists [14]. SUMO is owned by IEEE (Institute of Electrical and Electronics Engineers), and is freely available, subject to a usage license [15].

Careful study of SUMO would seem to indicate that the most carefully constructed ontologies are rife with inconsistencies, errors, and subtle traps for unworldly data scientists. For example, consider these two classes, both of which happen to be subclasses of Class Substance.

Subclass NaturalSubstance
Subclass SyntheticSubstance

It would seem that these two subclasses are mutually exclusive. However, diamonds occur naturally, and diamonds can be synthesized. Hence, diamond belongs to Subclass NaturalSubstance and to Subclass SyntheticSubstance. The ontology creates two mutually exclusive classes that contain some of the same objects; and this is a problem. We cannot create sensible inference rules for an object that occupies multiple, mutually exclusive classes.

Did the SUMO ontologists make a mistake? Maybe. Ontologies, unlike classifications, allow multiclass assignments (see Glossary item, Multiclass inheritance). A diamond can be a member of more than one class. Furthermore, there are no general rules for ontologies that disqualify dual membership in mutually exclusive classes. Still, those who use ontologies may prefer an alternate construction.

At first glance, the concepts "NaturalSubstance" and "SyntheticSubstance" would appear to be subclasses of "Substance." Are they really? Would it not be better to think that being "natural" or being "synthetic" are just properties of substances; not types of substances. Perhaps the most common mistake among ontologists is to confuse a subclass with a class property. If we agree that diamonds are a member of class substance, we can say that any specific diamond may have occurred naturally or through synthesis. We can eliminate two subclasses (i.e., "NaturalSubstance" and "SyntheticSubstance") and replace them with two properties of class "Substance": synthetic and natural. By assigning properties to a class of objects, we simplify the ontology (by reducing the number of subclasses), and we eliminate problems created when a class member belongs to two mutually exclusive subclasses.

SUMO contains many examples of objects assigned to multiple classes, causing some confusion. For example, in SUMO, humans are assigned to two different parent classes: Class Hominid and Class CognitiveAgent. "HumanCorpse," another SUMO class, is defined in SUMO as "A dead thing which was formerly a Human." Human corpse is a subclass of Class OrganicObject; not of Class Human. This means that a human, once it ceases to live, transits to a class that is not directly related to the class of humans. Basically, a member of Class Human will change its class and its ancestral lineage, at different timestamped moments. How does a data scientist deal with class objects that disappear from their assigned class and reappear elsewhere, over time?

Here is one more SUMO oddity. SUMO assigns algae as a subclass of nonflowering plant. It happens that algae are a diverse group of organisms that belong to several different classes of organisms. Diatoms, brown algae, golden algae, yellow-green algae all belong to Class Heterokonta. Blue-green algae belong to Class Bacteria. Green algae and red algae belong to Class Archaeplastida, a superclass of the nonflowering plants. There is no way of assigning a biologically diverse group of organisms to a class. Moreover, some algae are not nonflowering plants, their SUMO-assigned class. In summary, SUMO misclassifies the algae about as badly as anything can be misclassified.

Let us look at an example wherein scientists benefited by applying a classification to a repurposed dataset.

Case Study 6.6: Population Sampling by Class

Molecular biologists devote a great deal of effort toward sequencing the genome of bacterial species. With such knowledge, they hope to understand the pathways and genetic mechanisms that drive bacterial life. Because there are millions of species of bacteria, scientists cannot hope to isolate and sequence all of them. Hence, they must choose a sample of bacteria species with which to work, hoping that they can generalize their findings to other species.

What bacterial species should they sample? The standard operating procedure has been to select species based on some useful property (e.g., bacteria known to cause disease, bacteria known to synthesize particular molecular compounds of interest). As a result, scientists have data on a variety of interesting species, but the species do not adequately represent the known classes of bacterial organisms. Hence, observations on species in the database will apply to the particular species studied, but most findings will not be generalizable to classes of organisms.

It has been recently shown that when bacteria are selected to maximize phylogenetic coverage (i.e., choosing species that better represent the full class hierarchy of bacteria), the results of data analyses lead to improved predictions of functionality, that extend to organisms that are not included in the database [16].

Flawless classifications are seldom encountered. The most competent ontologists are likely to make mistakes, and most mistakes can be rectified over time. It is worth remembering that the classification of living organisms has been a work in progress for over 2,000 years. Scientists trust the current classification of living organisms, because they know that it is constantly being tested, criticized, and corrected. Scientists commit an unforgivable sin when they assume that any classification or ontology is a faithful and accurate representation of reality.

If classifications are difficult to construct, and if they are prone to flaws, then are they really worth creating? Might we not be good data scientists without access to classifications? The following case study illustrates some of the obstacles to progress that arise when scientists generate measurements on unclassified objects.

Case Study 6.7: What May Happen When There Is No Classification?

The past half century has seen remarkable advances in the field of brain imaging, including the introduction of computed tomography and nuclear magnetic resonance imaging. Scientists can now determine the brain areas that are selectively activated for specific physiologic functions. These imaging techniques include: positron emission tomography, functional magnetic resonance imaging, multichannel electroencephalography, magnetoencephalography, near-infrared spectroscopic imaging, and single photon emission computed tomography. With all of these available technologies, you would naturally expect that neuroscientists would be able to correlate psychiatric conditions with abnormalities in anatomy or function, mapped to specific areas of the brain. Indeed, the brain research literature has seen hundreds, if not thousands of early studies purporting to find associations that link brain anatomy to psychiatric diseases. Alas, none of these early findings have been validated. Excluding degenerative brain conditions (e.g., Alzheimer disease, Parkinson disease), there is, at the present time, no known psychiatric condition that can be consistently associated with a specific functional brain deficit or anatomic abnormality [17]. The reasons for the complete lack of validation for what seemed to be a highly promising field of research, pursued by an army of top scientists, is a disturbing mystery.

The year 2013 marked the arrival of a new version of the Diagnostic and Statistical Manual of Mental Disorders (DSM). The DSM is the standard classification of psychiatric disorders and is used by psychiatrists and other healthcare professionals worldwide. The new version was long in coming, following its previous version by 20 years. Spoiling the fanfare for the much-anticipated update was a chorus of loud detractors, who included among their ranks a host of influential and respected neuroscientists. Their complaint was that the DSM classifies diagnostic entities based on collections of symptoms; not on biological principles. For every diagnostic entity in the DSM, all persons who share the same collection of symptoms will, in most cases, be assigned the same diagnosis; even when the biological cause of the symptoms is unrelated.

Here is the problem, in a nutshell. Scientific observations on sampled populations can have scientific validity only when the objects in the sampled population are of the same type. If persons with unrelated diseases are studied together, simply because they have some symptoms in common, the results of the study are unlikely to have any validity. Dr. Thomas Insel, who at that time was Director of the National Institute of Mental Health, was quoted as saying "As long as the research community takes the DSM to be a bible, we'll never make progress" [18].

If scientists do not have a biologically valid classification of psychiatric illnesses, all of the studies using advanced imaging technology, and producing abundant and precise data, will have no value, because the patients being studied will not represent groups of people that have the same biological disease. Likewise, clinical trials for new and effective drugs for individuals with psychiatric diseases are unlikely to produce consistent results, if the persons enrolled in the trial have biologically separable conditions.

Data repurposing often starts with a classification of data objects. If the classification is deeply flawed, the repurposing project is likely to fail. Is there any occasion when a data scientist would **not** need to classify the objects within the data domain under study? Yes. When all of the objects are of the same type, classifications have no value. If all electrons are the same, if every bar of soap can do the same job, if every Barbie doll is manufactured at the same factory, then the issues of classification become relatively unimportant. When the samples under study are diverse (e.g., the hundred million different species of animals on the planet), then the data scientist must be able to distinguish the different classes of animal, and the classes must obey the general rules of classification.

6.5 IDENTITY AND UNIQUENESS

I always wanted to be somebody, but now I realize I should have been more specific.

Lily Tomlin

Uniqueness is a very strange concept, especially when applied to the realm of data. For example, if I refer to the number 1, then I am referring to a unique number among other numbers (i.e., there is only one number 1). Yet the number 1 may apply to many different things (i.e., 1 left shoe, 1 umbrella, 1 prime number between 2 and 5). The number 1 makes very little sense to us until we know something about what it measures and the object to which the measurement applies (see Glossary item, Uniqueness).

If we say "part number 32027563 weighs 1 pound," then we are dealing with an assertion that makes sense. The assertion tells us that there is a unique thing, known as part number 32027563, which has a weight, and the weight has a measurement of 1 pound. The phrase "weighs 1 pound" has no meaning until it is associated with a unique object (i.e., part number 32027563). We have just created a so-called "triple," the embodiment of meaning in the field of computational semantics. A triple consists of a unique, identified object, matched to a pair of data and metadata (i.e., a data element and the description of the data element). Information experts use formal syntax to express triples as data structures (see Glossary items, Meaning, RDF, RDF Schema, Notation 3).

Today, when we want to establish the uniqueness of some object (e.g., a material object or a data record, or a data element), we bind the object to an identifier, and we take great pains to ensure that the identifier is not assigned to any other object, and that the association between the object and its unique number is never lost.

For manufactured objects, such as car engines, prosthetic implants, and guns, a unique number is engraved into the object, and a record is kept, associating the record of the object (e.g., production date, product batch) with the number. For informaticians, an object is unique if it holds an alphanumeric string that no other object holds.

We refer to uniquely assigned computer-generated character strings as "identifiers." As such, computer-generated identifiers are abstract constructs that do not need to embody any of the natural properties of the object. A long (e.g., 200 character length) character string consisting of randomly chosen numeric and alphabetic characters is an excellent identifier, because the chances of two individuals being assigned the same string are essentially zero.

There are various methods for generating and assigning unique identifiers to data objects [7,19–21] (see Glossary items, Identification, Identifier, One-way hash, Universally Unique Identifier, UUID). Some identification systems assign a group prefix to an identifier sequence that is unique for the members of the group. For example, a prefix for a research institute may be attached to every data object generated within the institute. If the prefix is registered in a public repository, data from the institute can be merged with data from other institutes, and the institutional source of the data object can always be determined. The value of prefixes, and other reserved namespace designations, can be undermined when implemented thoughtlessly (see Glossary item, Namespace).

Case Study 6.8: Faulty Identifiers

Peter Kuzmak, an information specialist who works with medical images, made an interesting observation concerning the nonuniqueness of identifiers that were thought to be unique [22]. Hospitals that use the DICOM (Digital Imaging and Communications in Medicine) image standard assign a unique object identifier to each image. Each identifier comes with a prefix consisting of a permanent, registered code for the institution and the department, and a suffix consisting of a number generated for an image, attached at the moment when the image is created.

A hospital may assign consecutive numbers to its images, appending these numbers to an object identifier that is unique for the institution and for the department within the institution. For example, the first image created with a CT scanner might be assigned an identifier consisting of the assigned code for institution and department, followed by a separator such as a hyphen, followed by "1."

In a worst case scenario, different instruments may assign consecutive numbers to images, independently of one another. This means that the CT scanner in room A may be creating the same identifier (institution/department prefix + image number) as the CT scanner in Room B, for images on different patients. This problem could be remedied by constraining each CT scanner to avoid using numbers assigned by any other CT scanner.

When image counting is done properly, and the scanners are constrained to assign unique numbers (not previously assigned by other scanners in the same institution), then each image may indeed have a unique identifier (institution/department prefix + image number). Nonetheless, problems will arise when the image service is reassigned to another department in the institution, or when departments merge, or when institutions merge. Each of these shifts produces a change in the prefix for the institution and department. If a consecutive numbering system is used, then you can expect to create duplicate identifiers if institutional prefixes are replaced after the institutions are merged. In this case, the old records in both of the merging institutions will be assigned the same prefix and will contain replicates among the consecutively numbered suffixes (e.g., image 1, image 2, etc.).

Yet another problem may occur if one unique object is provided with multiple different unique identifiers. For example, a software application may assign a DICOM image, received from a hospital, and carrying its own unique identifier, with a second unique identifier. Assigning a second identifier insulates the software vendor from bad identifiers that may have been produced by the referring hospital. In so doing, the image now has two different unique identifiers. At this point, which identifier should be used to attach the various data and metadata annotations that accrue to the image, over time? By redundantly layering unique identifiers onto a data object, the software vendor defeats the original intended purpose of identifying the image (i.e., unambiguously connecting a data object to its data).

Timestamping is a method by which we can distinguish different states, versions, or events that apply to unique objects.

Case Study 6.9: Timestamping Data

"Time is what keeps everything from happening at once." Ray Cummings in his 1922 novel, "The Girl in the Golden Atom"

Time is a type of identifier. There must be many thousands of "Mary Smiths" in the world, but there is probably only one Mary Smith that was born on a given date and time. If you can assign the time down to a small fraction of a second, then you can use the name and time to establish the unique identity of the individual.

In David Reed's 1978 doctoral thesis, at MIT, he developed the idea of annotating data objects with timing data [23]. He described objects that were modifiable as a temporal sequence of immutable versions of the object (see Glossary item, Immutability). To understand this concept, consider height measurements on a growing child.

Alexander Goodboy, age 3 years, 34 inches height
Alexander Goodboy, age 5 years, 42 inches height
Alexander Goodboy, age 7 years, 46 inches height
Alexander Goodboy, age 9 years, 52 inches height

As the child grows, he passes through an infinite series of heights. How do we preserve an object's immutability when its data values keep changing? We do it with time. Every version of Alexander Goodboy is annotated by a timestamp, and the net result is a unique and immutable data object encapsulating many different timestamped heights.

All computers have an internal clock that coordinates operations (i.e., calculations), and the internal clock cycles can be synchronized to measurements of real time. This means that all computer events, including the acquisition of new versions of data values for unique and immutable objects (e.g., heights), can be timestamped.

All good legacy data is timestamped. Surprisingly, ancient scribes were fastidious timestampers. It would be an unusual Sumerian, Egyptian, or Mayan document that lacked an inscribed date. In contrast, it is easy to find modern, web-based news reports that lack any clue to the date that the webpage was created. Likewise, it is unusual to find spreadsheet data wherein the individual cells are timestamped. Much of our modern, electronic data, is insufficiently annotated.

Datasets that lack timestamps, unique identifiers, and metadata cannot be repurposed by anyone other than the data creator, who may have intimate knowledge of how the data was created and what the data means. Data has no value if it cannot be verified and validated by independent scientists. Datasets without annotations are little better than mindless doodles. In the following section, we shall discuss some of the negative consequences of omitting timestamp annotation.

6.6 WHEN TO TERMINATE (OR RECONSIDER) A DATA REPURPOSING PROJECT

Not everything that counts can be counted, and not everything that can be counted counts.

William Bruce Cameron

The most valuable features of data worth repurposing were described back in Section 2.5. Briefly, they are:

1. Data that establishes uniqueness or identity
2. Data that accrues over time, documenting the moments when data objects are obtained (i.e., timestamped data)
3. Data that establishes membership in a defined group or class
4. Data that is classified for every object in a knowledge domain
5. Introspective data—data that explains itself.

Another set of properties characterize datasets that are virtually useless for data repurposing projects.

1. Datasets that are incomplete or unrepresentative of the subject domain. You cannot draw valid conclusions, if the data you are analyzing is unrepresentative of the data domain under study.

   Having a large set of data does not guarantee that your data is complete and representative. Danah Boyd, a social media research, gives the example of a scientist who is analyzing the complete set of tweets made available by Twitter [24]. If Twitter removes tweets containing expletives, or tweets composed of nonword character strings, or tweets containing highly charged words, or tweets containing certain types of private information, then the resulting dataset, no matter how large it may be, is not representative of the population of senders (see Glossary item; Privacy vs. confidentiality). If the tweets are available as a set of messages, without any identifier for senders, then the compulsive tweeters (those who send hundreds or thousands of tweets) will be overrepresented, and the one-time tweeters will be underrepresented. If each tweet was associated with an account, and all the tweets from a single account were collected as a unique record, then there would still be the problem created by tweeters who maintain multiple accounts (see Glossary item, Representation bias).

   Contrariwise, having a small amount of data is not necessary fatal for data repurposing projects. If the data at hand cannot support your intended analysis, it may be sufficient to answer an alternate set of questions, particularly if the data indicate large effects and achieve statistical significance. In addition, small datasets can be merged with other small or large datasets to produce representative and complete aggregate data collections.

2. Data that lacks metadata. It may seem a surprise to some, but most of the data collected in the world today is poorly annotated. There is no way to determine how the data elements were obtained, or what they mean, and there is no way to verify the quality of the data.

3. Data without unique identifiers. If there is no way to distinguish data objects, then it impossible to distinguish 10 data values that apply to 1 object versus 10 data values that apply to 10 different objects.

   The term "identified data," a concept that is central to data science, must be distinguished from "data that is linked to an identified individual," a concept that has legal and ethical importance. In the privacy realm, the term, "data that is linked to an identified individual," is shortened to "identified data," and this indulgence has caused no end of confusion. Data can be deidentified only in the regulatory sense, by removing any links between the data and the person to whom the data applies (see Glossary items, Deidentification, Deidentification vs. anonymization, Reidentification). The data itself should never be stripped of an identifier string (i.e., a unique alphanumeric identifier for every data object must exist). Removing links that connect the data object to an individual is all that is necessary for so-called privacy deidentification.

4. Undocumented data (e.g., data with no known creator, or no known owner, or with no "rights" statement indicating who may use the data and for what purposes). Data scientists cannot assume that they can legally use every dataset that they acquire.

5. Illegal data or legally encumbered data or unethical data. Data scientists cannot assume that they have no legal liability when they use data that was appropriated unlawfully.

Data quality is serious business. The US government passed the Data Quality Act in 2001, as part of the FY 2001 Consolidated Appropriations Act (Pub. L. No. 106-554, see Glossary item, Data Quality Act). The Act requires Federal Agencies to base their policy decisions on high-quality data and to permit the public to challenge and correct inaccurate data [25,26]. The drawback to this legislation is that science is a messy process, and data may not always attain a high quality. Data that fails to meet standards of quality may be rejected by government committees or may be used to abrogate policies that were based on the data [27,28].

Data scientists may become overly fastidious with their data, rejecting opportunities to pursue important lines of inquiry when the data is not to their liking. For example, outliers and missing data values are the bane of statisticians (see Glossary item, Outlier). Nonetheless, data scientists should appreciate that anomalous data values can be overlooked clues, telling us what the data really means.

Case Study 6.10: Nonsensical Mayan Glyphs

For decades, work on decoding Mayan glyphs was stalled because translators could not find consistent glyph symbols for known Mayan words. To the first linguists who studied the Mayan glyphs, the stunning inconsistencies in glyphic symbols, at equivalent locations in Mayan scripts, suggested to them that the glyphs were elaborate doodles, not words.

As it turned out, the early linguists were completely mistaken. The glyph pictures were assemblages of syllabic symbols, and each syllable could be represented by a wide variety of equivalent symbols. The pictogram of a syllable, appearing inside a word glyph, was derived from the beginning sound produced when any of several alternate words were spoken.

If similar rules of word construction held for the English language, we might see the word "pal," meaning friend, spelled logophonetically with a string of pictures:

"PAL" = Puppy + Alaska + Lake (i.e., a montage consisting of a photo of a cute puppy, the outline of the state of Alaska, and a picture of a pristine lake)

Or

"PAL" = Pizza + Ant + Lips (i.e., a montage consisting of a picture of a slice of pizza, a crawling ant, and the silhouette of kissing lips).

If we studied the two montages, both representing the word "pal," we might conclude that the montage images could not possibly represent the same word. We would be wrong. Sometimes, our best data is apparently inconsistent and nonsensical.

We have seen examples of seemingly hopeless datasets that proved to have great value to data repurposers. A good data munger can often restore structure to unstructured data, create values for missing data elements by imputation, reduce the complexity of highly dimensional data, use mean field averaging techniques to simplify computations on dense datasets, follow and predict trends in sparse but timestamped data, transform heterogenous data types to a common model, and otherwise compensate for a host of data-related sins (see Glossary items, Data reduction, Transform, Fourier series, Principal component analysis, Dimensionality, Curse of dimensionality, Mean-field approximation) [29−31].

Case Study 6.11: Flattened Data

Data flattening is a term that is used differently by data analysts, database experts, and informaticians. Though the precise meaning changes from subfield to subfield, the term always seems to connote a simplification of the data and the elimination of unnecessary structural restraints.

In the field of informatics, data flattening is a popular but ultimately counterproductive method of data organization and data reduction. Data flattening involves removing data annotations that are not needed for the interpretation of data.

Imagine, for the sake of illustration, a drastic option that was seriously considered by a large medical institution. This institution, that shall remain nameless, had established an excellent Electronic Medical Record (EMR) system. The EMR assigns a unique and permanent identifier string to each patient and attaches the identifier string to every hospital transaction involving the patient (e.g., biopsy reports, pharmacy reports, nursing notes, laboratory reports). All of the data relevant to a patient produced anywhere within the hospital system is linked by the patient's unique identifier. The patient's EMR can be assembled, instantly, whenever needed, via a database query.

Over time, the patient records in well-designed information systems accrue a huge number of annotations (e.g., timestamped data elements, object identifiers, linking elements, metadata). The database manager is saddled with the responsibility of maintaining the associations among all of the annotations. For example, an individual with a particular test, conducted at a particular time, on a particular day, will have annotations that link the test to a test procedure protocol, an instrument identifier, a test code, a laboratory name, a test sample, a sample accession time, and so on. If data objects could be stripped of most of their annotations, after some interval of time, then it would reduce the overall data management burden on the hospital information system. This can be achieved by composing simplified reports and deleting the internal annotations. For example, all of the data relevant to a patient's laboratory test could be reduced to the patient's name, the date, the name of the test, and the test result. All of the other annotations can be deleted. This process is called data flattening.

Should a medical center, or any entity that collects data, flatten their data? The positive result would be a streamlining of the system, with a huge reduction in annotation overhead. The negative result would be the loss of the information that connects well-defined data objects (e.g., test result with test protocol, test instrument with test result, name of laboratory technician with test sample, name of clinician with name of patient). Because the fundamental activity of the data scientist is to find relationships among data objects, data flattening will reduce the scope and value of data repurposing projects. Without annotations and metadata, the data from different information systems cannot be sensibly merged. Furthermore, if there is a desire or a need to reanalyze flattened data, then the data scientist will not be able to verify the data and validate the conclusions drawn from the data (see Glossary items, Verification, Validation).

Every data scientist should understand that there comes a time when she must say "I give up. This data is just garbage." Optimists would argue that there are many examples of data problems that were once deemed intractable, only to be solved by a new set of analysts, with a fresh approach. Hence, when terminating a project, it is best to pack up cleanly and with adequate documentation. Save the data! Allow other scientists the chance to succeed, one day, where you have failed.

REFERENCES

[1] Curry A. Rescue of old data offers lesson for particle physicists. Science 2011;331:694–5.

[2] Biebel O, Movilla Fernandez PA, Bethke S, the JADE Collaboration. C-parameter and jet broadening at PETRA energies. Phys Lett 1999;B459:326–34.

[3] Meyer R. A long-lost spacecraft, now saved, faces its biggest test yet. Atlantic June 3, 2014.

[4] FIPS PUB 119-1. Supersedes FIPS PUB 119. 1985 November 8. Federal Information Processing Standards Publication 119-1 1995 March 13. Announcing the Standard for ADA. Available from: <http://www.itl.nist.gov/fipspubs/fip119-1.htm> [accessed 26.08.12].

[5] National Committee on Vital and Health Statistics. Report to the Secretary of the U.S. Department of Health and Human Services on Uniform Data Standards for Patient Medical Record Information. Available from: <http://www.ncvhs.hhs.gov/hipaa000706.pdf> [accessed 06.07.00].

[6] Kammer RG. The Role of Standards in Today's Society and in the Future. Statement of Raymond G. Kammer, Director, National Institute of Standards and Technology, Technology Administration, Department of Commerce, Before the House Committee on Science Subcommittee on Technology, September 13, 2000.

[7] Berman JJ. Principles of big data: preparing, sharing, and analyzing complex information. Burlington, MA: Morgan Kaufmann; 2013.

[8] Duncan M. Terminology version control discussion paper: the chocolate teapot. Medical Object Oriented Software Ltd.; September 15, 2009. Available from: <http://www.mrtablet. demon.co.uk/chocolate_teapot_lite.htm>[accessed 30.08.12].

[9] Berman JJ, Moore GW. Implementing an RDF Schema for Pathology Images 2007. Available from: <http://www.julesberman.info/spec2img.htm> [accessed 01.01.15].

[10] Pearson K. The grammar of science. London: Adam and Black; 1900.

[11] Berman JJ. Taxonomic guide to infectious diseases: understanding the biologic classes of pathogenic organisms. Waltham: Academic Press; 2012.

[12] Scamardella JM. Not plants or animals: a brief history of the origin of Kingdoms Protozoa, Protista and Protoctista. Int Microbiol 1999;2:207−16.

[13] Patil N, Berno AJ, Hinds DA, Barrett WA, Doshi JM, Hacker CR, et al. Blocks of limited haplotype diversity revealed by high-resolution scanning of human chromosome 21. Science 2001;294:1719−23.

[14] Niles I, Pease A. Towards a standard upper ontology. In: Welty C, Smith B, editors. Proceedings of the second international conference on formal ontology in information systems (FOIS-2001), Ogunquit, Maine, October 17−19, 2001.

[15] Suggested Upper Merged Ontology (SUMO). The OntologyPortal. Available from: <http:// www.ontologyportal.org> [accessed 14.08.12].

[16] Wu D, Hugenholtz P, Mavromatis K, Pukall R, Dalin E, Ivanova NN, et al. A phylogeny-driven genomic encyclopaedia of Bacteria and Archaea. Nature 2009;462:1056−60.

[17] Borgwardt S, Radua J, Mechelli A, Fusar-Poli P. Why are psychiatric imaging methods clinically unreliable? Conclusions and practical guidelines for authors, editors and reviewers. Behav Brain Funct 2012;8:46.

[18] Belluck P, Carey B. Psychiatry's guide is out of touch with science, experts say. The New York Times May 6, 2013.

[19] Leach P, Mealling M, Salz R. A universally unique identifier (UUID) URN namespace. Network Working Group, Request for Comment 4122, Standards Track. Available from: <http://www.ietf.org/rfc/rfc4122.txt> [accessed 01.01.15].

[20] Mealling M. RFC 3061. A URN namespace of object identifiers. Network Working Group; 2001. Available from: <https://www.ietf.org/rfc/rfc3061.txt> [accessed 01.01.15].

[21] Berman JJ. Methods in medical informatics: fundamentals of healthcare programming in perl, python, and ruby. Boca Raton, FL: Chapman and Hall; 2010.

[22] Kuzmak P, Casertano A, Carozza D, Dayhoff R, Campbell K. Solving the Problem of Duplicate Medical Device Unique Identifiers High Confidence Medical Device Software and Systems (HCMDSS) Workshop, Philadelphia, PA, June 2−3, 2005. Available from: <http:// www.cis.upenn.edu/hcmdss/Papers/submissions/> [accessed 26.08.12].

[23] Reed DP. Naming and synchronization in a decentralized computer system (Doctoral Thesis). MIT; 1978.

[24] Boyd D. 2010. Privacy and Publicity in the Context of Big Data. Open Government and the World Wide Web (WWW2010), Raleigh, NC, April 29, 2010. Available from: <http://www. danah.org/papers/talks/2010/WWW2010.html> [accessed 26.08.12].

[25] Data Quality Act. 67 Fed. Reg. 8,452, February 22, 2002, addition to FY 2001 Consolidated Appropriations Act (Pub. L. No. 106-554. codified at 44 U.S.C. 3516).

[26] Guidelines for ensuring and maximizing the quality, objectivity, utility, and integrity of information disseminated by federal agencies. Fed Regist 2002;67(36).

[27] Sass JB, Devine Jr. JP. The Center for Regulatory Effectiveness invokes the Data Quality Act to reject published studies on atrazine toxicity. Environ Health Perspect 2004;112:A18.

[28] Tozzi JJ, Kelly Jr WG, Slaughter S. Correspondence: data quality act: response from the Center for Regulatory Effectiveness. Environ Health Perspect 2004;112:A18−19.

[29] Janert PK. Data analysis with open source tools. Sebastopol, CA: O'Reilly Media; 2010.

[30] Carpenter JR, Kenward MG. Missing data in randomised control trials: a practical guide. November 21, 2007. Available from: <http://www.hta.nhs.uk/nihrmethodology/reports/1589. pdf> [28.06.11].

[31] Bache R, Miles S, Coker B, Taweel A. Informative provenance for repurposed data: a case study using clinical research data. Int J Digit Curation 2013;8:27−46.

CHAPTER 7

Social and Economic Issues

7.1 DATA SHARING AND REPRODUCIBLE RESEARCH

In God we trust, all others bring data.

William Edwards Deming (1900–1993)

In a simpler time, a scientist would perform an experiment in his laboratory, record the results, draw some conclusion, and publish a manuscript that summarized the findings. Skeptics could repeat the same experiment, in their own laboratories, to confirm the results. Most experiments were simple affairs, and scientists took pains to ensure that their work was reproducible, before committing to publication. It was rare for a manuscript to be publicly discredited.

In today's "big science" world, tasks are distributed to many different laboratories, that use sophisticated equipment to collect gigabytes and terabytes of data. Such experiments cannot be repeated. The only way to validate such large and complex experiments is to share the data, along with the protocols by which the data was generated and collected.

The past decade has witnessed a social movement towards data sharing. The U.S. National Academy of Sciences has called for scientists to provide publishers with the primary data that supports their conclusions [1,2]. For the data scientist who hopes to repurpose preexisting data, getting access to published data is crucial.

Case Study 7.1: Sharing Public-Funded Research Data with the Public

For those investigators who are funded by their governments, the obligation to share their data comes from public rights considerations. If the public has funded a researcher, shouldn't the results of the research, in the form of data and manuscripts, be freely available to the public? Must the public pay publishers for access to research that the public has sponsored? The leadership at the U.S. National Institutes of Health developed a policy intended to provide NIH-funded research to the public, at no cost. In 2005, the U.S. National Institutes of Health asked NIH-funded investigators to voluntarily deposit a copy of their published manuscripts in a government repository (i.e., PubMed Central) that would be made freely and openly available to the public. Investigator compliance with this new policy was dismal, with voluntary contributions coming from about 2.3% of government-funded investigators [3]. Noncompliance was attributed to a variety of obstacles, such as technical difficulties, labor and expenses of compliance, and prior contractual obligations to publishers. In truth, none of these obstacles were particularly daunting. The salient reason for noncompliance stemmed from the traditional attitude, held for centuries, that scientists own the data that they produce. Scientists may hoard their data to put themselves into the strongest position to exploit their studies for their own gain or to defend themselves against potential detractors. Data hoarding, also called data withholding, is, to this day, a common practice among scientists [4].

Several years of poor compliance passed. In 2008, the NIH issued a new data-sharing policy; this one would be mandatory [5]. Since the new policy came into effect, the aforementioned obstacles to data sharing seem to have vanished, and compliance has soared. Along with their manuscripts, NIH-funded scientists are strongly encouraged to submit all of the primary data supporting their conclusions. It would be hard to find any entity on this planet that has shared more data, with the public, than the U.S. Government.

7.2 ACQUIRING AND STORING DATA

This section is written with the caveat that the author is not a lawyer; what follows should not be taken as legal advice. Nonetheless, there is good news for data scientists seeking publicly available legacy data. With only certain unusual exceptions, raw data is not protected by Copyright law. Copyright is designed to protect creative works, not recordings of fact. Hence, in most cases, if you can lay your hands on a publicly available collection of raw data, then you can freely use that data without fear of violating Copyright. This holds true generally, even when the data is extracted from a document, a compilation, or a book that is itself protected from Copyright. In these cases, the form in which the raw data is held (e.g., its arrangement in a published book), is protected; the raw data is not.

There are exceptions to the general rule. Exceptions, for the most part, depend on whether any intellectual effort was involved to produce the facts or the specific form in which the facts must be used. Such exceptions might include cases wherein the data owner creatively selected the data, or in cases wherein the data owner had transformed the data using a creative method of her own design, or in cases wherein the data could not be understood without the benefit of a customized database created by the data owner [6].

Case Study 7.2: What Is Protected Data?

The distinction between form and content (i.e., bare facts vs. intellectual property) was made in the 1991 U.S. Supreme Court Case of *Feist Publishing, Inc. v. Rural Telephone Service Co*. When Rural Telephone Co. refused to license their alphabetized listing of names and telephone numbers to Feist Publishing, Inc., Feist proceeded to copy and use the data. Rural Telephone Co. claimed copyright infringement. In addition, Rural Telephone Co. argued that much effort went into collecting the individual records (name, address, and telephone number). Rural Telephone Co. asked the court to protect their data under the "sweat of brow" doctrine (i.e., holdings acquired by an individual's efforts merited legal protection). The Supreme Court rejected both arguments, deciding that raw data included in a copyright document is not protected by copyright, and that raw data, having no creative input, was not protected by the "sweat of brow" doctrine.

European courts differ somewhat from American courts with regard to database protections. Like their American counterparts, Europeans interpret copyright to cover creative works, not data collections. However, the 1996 European Database Directive instructs courts to extend sui generis (i.e., one of a kind or exceptional) protection to databases. In Europe, databases that may have required a significant investment of time, effort, and money cannot be freely copied for commercial use.

What is the moral of this story? In general, the safest legacy data is public data that has not been modified from its raw (i.e., directly measured) values. If the data has been made available to the public, and if its public presence is not contestable, and if there are no explicit restrictions on its use, then it can be assumed that the data is intended to be used by the public. If the data is raw, not improved, not filtered, and not transformed through some nonobvious algorithm or through the creative application of the selective process, then the data is non-creative and not generally subject to copyright protection.

7.3 KEEPING YOUR DATA FOREVER

Legacy data requires perpetual storage. How is that accomplished? The simplest solution involves making redundant copies. At first blush, it would be hard to argue that redundancy, in the context of information systems, is a bad thing. With redundancy, when one server fails, another takes up the slack. If a software system crashes, its duplicate takes over; when one file is lost, it is replaced by its backup copy. The problem with redundancy is that it makes the system much more complex by creating a new set of interdependencies.

A stunning example of a failed redundant system involved the Japanese nuclear power plant at Fukushima. The plant was designed with redundant systems. If the power failed, a backup generator would kick in. On March 11, 2011, a powerful earthquake off the shore of Japan produced a tidal wave that cut the nuclear reactor's access to the electric power grid. The backup generators were flooded by the same tidal wave. The consequent meltdown and radiation leaks created the worst nuclear disaster since Chernobyl.

Redundancy is employed in computer systems that cannot be allowed to fail. On June 4, 1996, the first flight of the Ariane 5 rocket self-destructed, 37 seconds after launch. There was a bug in the software, but the Ariane had been fitted with a backup computer. The backup was no help; the same bug that crippled the primary computer put the redundant backup computer out of business [7].

Nature has an ambivalent attitude toward redundant systems. Humans evolved to have two eyes, two arms, two legs, two kidneys, and so on. Not every organ comes in duplicate. We have one heart, one brain, one liver, one spleen. There are no organs that come in triplicate. A spear that slices through a kidney is likely to spare the second kidney, but a systemic poison that causes toxicity in one organ will be equally toxic to the contralateral twin.

Case Study 7.3: A Backup That Backfired

What is the best way to save large legacy datasets? One of the most popular methods of storing data is through the venerable off-site backup. If, for any reason, the data is destroyed or corrupted at the primary data site, then the backup data can be retrieved and the original data restored.

The drawback of this approach is that the backup files create a security risk. In Portland Oregon, in 2006, 365,000 medical records were stolen from Providence Home Services, a division of Seattle-based Providence Health Systems [8]. The thief was an employee who was simply given the backup files and instructed to store them in his home, as a security measure. In essence, the thief was instructed, by the data owner, to take all the data. In this case, a plan to create a safe, off-site backup, resulted in a major security breach.

Today, the concept of a data collection, stored at a single site, perhaps on a single server, is somewhat antiquated. More often, data is composed of uniquely identified data objects that may be distributed over geographically separated networks. Multiple copies of data objects can be created and stored at multiple locations. Furthermore, data can be easily encrypted to ensure that unauthorized persons who come into possession of the data will be unable to make any sense of the contents. The greatest challenges in the modern computing environment will come in the form of managing the complexity of data storage: keeping track of the data identifiers; establishing proper authorizations for data use; creating safe protocols whereby authorized entities (e.g., humans, software agents) can locate and decrypt data, as needed; ensuring the immutability and immortality of data.

7.4 DATA IMMUTABILITY

How is it that you keep mutating and can still be the same virus?
Chuck Palahniuk, in his novel, Invisible Monsters

Everyone is familiar with the iconic image, from Orwell's 1984, of a totalitarian government that watches its citizens from telescreens [9]. The ominous phrase "Big Brother is watching you" evokes an important thesis of Orwell's masterpiece; that a totalitarian government can use an expansive surveillance system to crush the enemies of the state.

Orwell's book had a second thesis that was much more insidious and much more disturbing than the threat of intrusive surveillance. Orwell was concerned that governments could change the past and the present by inserting, deleting, and otherwise distorting the information available to citizens [10]. In Orwell's 1984, old reports of military defeats, genocidal atrocities, ineffective policies, mass starvation, and any ideas that might foment unrest among the proletariat were deleted and replaced with propaganda pieces. In Orwell's dystopian world, retrospective data-altering activities distorted humanity's perception of reality to suit a totalitarian agenda. Today, our perception of reality can be altered by deleting or modifying electronic data distributed via the internet.

Case Study 7.4: Retrospective Deletion of Data

In 2009, Amazon was eagerly selling electronic editions of a popular book, much to the displeasure of the book's publisher. Amazon, to mollify the publisher, did something that seemed impossible. Amazon retracted the electronic books from the devices of readers who had already made their purchase. Where there was once a book on a personal ebook reader, there was now nothing. Amazon compensated the customers by crediting their accounts for the price of the book. So far as Amazon and the publisher were concerned, the equilibrium of the world was restored [11].

The public reaction to Amazon's vanishing act was a combination of bewilderment ("What just happened?"), shock ("How was it possible for Amazon to do this?"), outrage ("That book was mine!"), fear ("What else can they do to my ebook reader?"), and suspicion ("Can I ever buy another ebook?"). Amazon quickly apologized for any misunderstanding and promised not to do it again.

To add an element of irony to the episode, the book that was acquired, then deleted, to suit the needs of a powerful entity, was George Orwell's 1984.

In a connected, digital world it is relatively easy to experiment on individuals, without their permission or awareness.

Case Study 7.5: Reality Tampering

In 2012, Facebook conducted an experiment on nearly 700,000 individuals, by manipulating their aggregated news feeds. One group was selectively sent sad and depressing news items. The other group was sent aggregated news feeds with content that was more upbeat. Facebook wanted to determine whether an onslaught of mind-numbing news might influence the tone of the Facebook posts that followed [12].

News of the study evoked public outrage. Human subjects had been enrolled in an experiment without their consent and without their awareness. The information received by these unknowing human subjects had been manipulated to produce a distorted perception of reality. The experimental results, in the form of Facebook posts written by the subjects, had been monitored by data analysts [12,13].

Following the outrage came a corporate apology. Academics, some of whom participated in the project, are now leading discussions with other academics, to develop ethical guidelines [12].

We have all been entertained by stories of time travel wherein a protagonist is sent into the past, to stop some horrible event from happening. A series of improbable misadventures spoils the fun, proving that the past cannot be altered. We humans are enthralled with the prospect of obliterating the bad things in our lives.

Case Study 7.6: Case Study: The Dubious Right to be Forgotten

The European Court of Justice, in a directive handed down in May 2014, decided that skeletons are best kept in closets. The court asked Google to remove the links, from European domains, to a 1998 article that contained material that was embarrassing; but factual, for the claimant [14]. On the first day of Google's compliance with the Court's directive, Google received 12,000 additional requests to remove links to other web pages.

When a website is delinked by Google, the content of the site is not altered. What changes is that the site will no longer appear in Google search results. For practical purposes, the site will be forgotten. Hence, the right to be delinked from Google, under the European Court's directive, is glibly referred to as the right to be forgotten.

If there is widespread delinking of internet sites, or if the process escalates, to involve the forced removal of materials by internet providers, then the universe of information will become mutable, changing from moment to moment. Individuals will argue that they have the right to be forgotten. Data scientists will argue that the right to be forgotten is actually the right to alter reality.

7.5 PRIVACY AND CONFIDENTIALITY

Never answer an anonymous letter.

Yogi Berra

Confidentiality and privacy are two related but separable concepts. Confidentiality is about keeping a secret. If you reveal a secret told in confidence, then you are breaching confidentiality. Privacy is about intrusions into a person's private life. If you come upon someone's unlisted phone number, and you call him at night, without his permission, then you are breaching privacy.

In the information universe, confidentiality issues center on the unwanted distribution of information that was provided in confidence (e.g., medical histories, social security numbers). Computer privacy issues often center on computer invasions (i.e., turning a laptop's webcam into a spying device, unauthorized access beyond an individual's firewall).

Data scientists occasionally need access to large datasets that may contain confidential information, or information that could be used to invade the privacy of individuals. In this case, the most reasonable way to protect individuals may involve removing all data that could be linked to an individual. This process, described in Section 6.6, is called deidentification. The principle underlying the effectiveness of deidentification is that if confidential data cannot be linked to an individual, then it cannot harm the individual.

Aside from issues linking confidential data to an identified individual, other issues of confidentiality and privacy may apply. As an exercise, let's consider a few hypothetical situations.

1. "Sally Smith," "glucose level in mg/dL," "85"
   Note, this record is provided in the form of a triple, consisting of the name of an object, followed by metadata, followed by data. We could deidentify the record by removing "Sally Smith," thus creating a disembodied metadata/data pair, that could be used by data analysts, without violating Sally Smith's medical confidentiality.
2. "Sally Smith," "unlisted phone number," "1-234-567-8910"
   We could try to deidentify the record by removing "Sally Smith," but if a criminal had access to a reverse telephone directory for unlisted numbers, he could learn that the telephone number belonged to Sally Smith.
   The reason why the phone number in this example, unlike the glucose level in the prior example, is a potential identifier is that the telephone number is unique. It only rings one telephone, Sally Smith's. A glucose value of 85 is not unique, applying to billions of individuals.

3. "Sally Smith" "murdered," "Colonel Mustard."

Here, if we removed Sally Smith's name, her confidentiality would be protected. Still the remaining set of metadata/data would be incriminating, as it would indicate that Colonel Mustard had been murdered. We might eliminate Colonel Mustard's name, but we would still have an incriminating piece of metadata, indicating that someone had been murdered.

In examples 2 and 3, we see instances in which data can be deidentified, yet still contain information that is private, and potentially harmful to individuals. After all of the identifiers in a dataset are removed, conditions may persist wherein data should not be freely shared.

The removal of all objectionable data from a document or a dataset is referred to a data scrubbing. There are two general algorithmic approaches to scrubbing data. The first is a rule-based approach wherein the programmer attempts to foresee all of the general patterns of confidential or private data, writing short routines that remove any fragments of data that match the patterns. For example, a routine may delete any character sequences that match the general form of a telephone number or a social security number or a calendar date. The program might delete the capitalized words that immediately follow honorifics (e.g., Mr, Mrs, Ms, Dr). These algorithms often contain hundreds of rules, but they never seem to extract all of the identifiers or private material. Additionally, such algorithms are extremely slow, as they must test each line of text against every rule. A second algorithmic approach is to sweep clean every piece of data, except for the data that has been certified as "clean."

Case Study 7.7: Text Scrubber

The concept-match or doublet-match algorithm and closely related methods have been described [10,15−17]. All versions of the algorithm involve a text or dataset to be scrubbed, and a list of approved terms that are considered to have no identifying value and no privacy value (i.e., the "safe" list). The text to be scrubbed is parsed, word-by-word. When a sequence of words in the text or dataset is encountered that matches any of the terms in the "safe" list, the sequence is preserved. Fragments of text that do not match a "safe" term are deleted. When the entire text or dataset has been parsed, the output is considered to be scrubbed of identifiers and private information, and can be shared with little chance of breaching confidentiality or privacy.

One of the best features of these list-based scrubbing algorithms is speed, executing thousands of times faster than rule-based scrubbing methods [17–19].

7.6 THE ECONOMICS OF DATA REPURPOSING

We live in an age of unprecedented technological progress, which is making everyone far more efficient than before. Yet where is the payoff?

Paul Krugman, economist [20]

Research is counterproductive when it attempts to discover things that have already been discovered, or when irrefutable principles are ignored. For example, the U.S. Patent and Trade Office has issued an official policy that prohibits new patent applications for perpetual motion machines. The office had received too many failed applications for silly devices that clearly violate the second law of thermodynamics. Enough is enough.

Outside the confines of the Patent Office, the wasted efforts of scientists cannot be halted by issuing a policy statement. All too often, scientific advancements are ignored or lost, and years are wasted before being rediscovered, at great expense. Examples of such lost and rediscovered treasures include the treatment of scurvy with foods rich in Vitamin C, the utility of handwashing in medical clinics, the technique of smallpox vaccination, and the importance of laying babies to sleep on their backs, not on their stomachs [16,21].

Case Study 7.8: Avoiding the Time Loop

Of the various kinds of experiments performed by medical researchers, randomized clinical trials are among the most expensive. It takes about 10–15 years to develop and market a new drug [22]. Only 5 in 5,000 compounds that have preclinical testing will enter clinical trials [22]. The cost of developing a drug and bringing it to market is about $1 billion [10].

Clinical trials are large and elaborate affairs, occasionally necessitating the enrollment of over 100,000 individuals [23]. Consequently, it can be difficult or impossible to enroll the required number of participants. In an analysis of 500 planned cancer trials, 40% of trials failed to accrue the minimum necessary number of patients [24]. After the trial, it may take years or decades to determine whether a treatment that demonstrated a small, but statistically significant effect in a clinical trial, will have equivalent value in everyday practice.

In a study conducted in 2005, a reanalysis of clinical trial literature found that a large number of clinical trials had been conducted to address questions that had already been definitively answered, before the trial began [25]. Clinical trialists and Institutional Review Boards, which approve the projects conducted within a research institution, had simply been unaware that their studies were redundant and pointless (i.e., they had ignored the existing legacy data).

Sometimes, the purpose of a data reanalysis is to determine when a scientific question has been adequately addressed. Have there been a sufficient number of high-quality studies, producing a reproducible and credible result, to say that further studies are unnecessary? As a rule, data repurposing projects are inexpensive and fast. A thoughtful and creative analysis of old data can sometimes save the enormous costs of a clinical trial.

Case Study 7.9: Bargain Basement Cancer Research

One of the more promising paradigms in cancer researcher rests on the premise that every type of cancer is preceded by another lesion known as a precancer [26]. In theory, if we treated all of the precancers that occur in humans, then we could stop the occurrence of all human cancers.

If the precancer paradigm was true, and every cancer was preceded by its precancer lesion, then the average age of occurrence of a precancer lesion, in a large population, must be earlier than the average age of occurrence of the cancer that eventually develops from the lesion. If we wanted to test this hypothesis, we could start today to build a patient database. As patients come into the system, with diagnoses of cancer or of the presumed precancer, we would record their ages. Eventually, we would have a sufficiently large collection of cases to say whether the peak of occurrence of precancers arrives in patients at an earlier age than the peak of occurrence of cancer. Collecting such data, on a large scale, would be a matter of great monetary expense and would require the participation of a small army of healthcare personnel and data managers.

Alternately, we can use collected clinical data to ask a question for which the data was not originally designed. The U.S. National Cancer Institute's Surveillance, Epidemiology and End Results (SEER) program provides individual deidentified records on a large number of U.S. Cancer patients. The SEER data is used to track the incidence of the various types of cancers, by year, and by geographic location. It is not designed to shed light on fundamental questions of cancer biology, but

SEER encourages the use of its data for any purpose that might reduce the burden of this horrible disease.

The SEER public data files covering years 1973–2005 also includes data on the so-called intraepithelial neoplasms of the uterine cervix, all of which are generally assumed to be the precursors of invasive cervical cancer [27]. Drawing from the preexisting SEER files, a short program produced the output shown below, in a matter of seconds [17].

```
Avg. Age at    Diagnosis
occurrence
------------------------------------------------
Precancers
   34 years    carcinoma in situ, nos
   34 years    squamous cell carcinoma in situ, nos
   35 years    sq. cell carcinoma, large cell, non-kerat, in situ
   37 years    sq. cell carcinoma, kerat, nos, in situ
   39 years    adenocarcinoma in situ
   39 years    squamous intraepithelial neoplasia, grade iii
Microinvasive cancer
   41 years    sq. cell carcinoma, micro-invasive
Fully invasive cancers
   49 years    sq. cell carcinoma, lg. cell, non-kerat
   51 years    sq. cell carcinoma, sm. cell, non-kerat
   51 years    sq. cell carcinoma, kerat, nos
   51 years    adenocarcinoma, nos
Abbreviations: nos = not otherwise specified, sq = squamous,
kerat = keratinizing [26].
```

Without dwelling on the specifics, the output shows that the average age of occurrence of the cervical precancers preceded the average age of occurrence of the cervical cancers, in every instance [26]. Overall, there is more than a 10-year gap between the average age of diagnosis of individuals who have the putative precancer lesions and the average age of diagnosis of individuals who have the fully invasive malignancies. This would imply that, on average, a cervical precancer will require more than 10 years to evolve into a cancer. Eliminating the precancer, at any time during this period, would prevent the occurrence of the invasive cancer [26,28–30]. This study was conducted in the space of a few hours, required no software other than Perl, created a new use for a venerable public dataset, and did not cost a penny.

Everyone knows that the world is awash with digital information. Although there is no way of knowing the total amount of time and money spent creating and managing all of this data, few would deny that the costs must be enormous. Perhaps it is time for a new generation of data scientists to find new purposes for old data. Based on the case studies appearing throughout this book, we can make a few tentative assertions, pertaining to the future of data repurposing:

1. Data repurposing will become more and more popular as we continue to collect and store large quantities of annotated, high-quality data.
2. Data repurposing efforts will produce faster research results, with a lower investment of capital.
3. The skill set necessary for repurposing legacy data is different from the skill set necessary for the original design and analysis of the data. Talented data scientists will forgo the resources wielded by corporations and governments, opting to work with preexisting data, as solo analysts or as consultants.
4. Data repurposing will accelerate scientific, technical, medical, and economic progress throughout the world.

It all seems a bit grandiose, but there is reason to be hopeful.

REFERENCES

[1] Sharing publication-related data and materials: responsibilities of authorship in the life sciences. The National Academies Press, Washington, DC, 2003. Available from: <http://www.nap.edu/openbook.php?isbn = 0309088593> [accessed 10.09.12].

[2] Neutra RR, Cohen A, Fletcher T, Michaels D, Richter ED, Soskolne CL. Epidemiology 2006;17(3):335–8.

[3] NIH Public Access Working Group of the NLM Board of Regents meeting summary, April 10, 2006.

[4] Vogeli C, Yucel R, Bendavid E, Jones LM, Anderson MS, Louis KS, et al. Data withholding and the next generation of scientists: results of a national survey. Acad Med 2006;81:128–36.

[5] Revised policy on enhancing public access to archived publications resulting from NIH-Funded Research. Notice Number: NOT-OD-08-033. Release date: January 11, 2008. Effective date: April 7, 2008. Available from: <http://grants.nih.gov/grants/guide/notice-files/not-od-08-033.html> [accessed 28.12.09].

[6] de Cock Buning M, Ringnalda A, van der Linden T. The legal status of raw data: a guide for research practice. SURF foundation, July 2009.

[7] Leveson NG. A new approach to system safety engineering. Self-published ebook; 2002.

[8] Weiss TR. Thief nabs backup data on 365,000 patients. Computerworld, January 26, 2006. Available from: http://www.computerworld.com/s/article/108101/Update_Thief_nabs_backup_data_on_365_000_patients [accessed 21.08.12].

[9] Orwell G. 1984. Signet, Tiptree, UK, 1950.

[10] Berman JJ. Principles of big data: preparing, sharing, and analyzing complex information. Burlington, MA: Morgan Kaufmann; 2013.

[11] Pogue D. Amazon.com plays big brother with famous e-books. The New York Times July 17, 2009.

[12] Goel V. As data overflows online, researchers grapple with ethics. The New York Times August 12, 2014.

[13] Sullivan G. Cornell ethics board did not pre-approve Facebook mood manipulation study Share on Facebook Share on Twitter Share on Google Plus Share via Email More Options.. The Washington Post July 1, 2014.

[14] O'Brien KJ. European court opinion favors google in privacy battle. The New York Times June 25, 2013.

[15] Berman JJ. Concept-match medical data scrubbing: how pathology datasets can be used in research. Arch Pathol Lab Med Arch Pathol Lab Med 2003;127:680−6.

[16] Berman JJ. Biomedical informatics. Sudbury, MA: Jones and Bartlett; 2007.

[17] Berman JJ. Methods in medical informatics: fundamentals of healthcare programming in perl, python, and ruby. Boca Raton, FL: Chapman and Hall; 2010.

[18] Berman JJ. Comparing de-identification methods. March 31, 2006. Available from: <http://www.biomedcentral.com/1472-6947/6/12/comments/comments.htm> [accessed 01.01.15].

[19] Berman JJ. Doublet method for very fast autocoding. BMC Med Inform Decis Mak 2004;4:16.

[20] Krugman P. The accidental theorist, and other dispatches from the dismal science. New York, NY: W.W. Norton; 1998. p. 101.

[21] Berman JJ. Machiavelli's laboratory. Amazon Digital Services, Inc.; 2010.

[22] Orphan drugs in development for rare diseases; 2011 Report. America's Biopharmaceutical Research Companies. Available from: <http://www.phrma.org/sites/default/files/pdf/rarediseases2011.pdf> [14.07.13].

[23] Prostate, lung, colorectal & ovarian cancer screening trial (PLCO). Available from: <http://prevention.cancer.gov/plco> [22.08.13].

[24] English R, Lebovitz Y, Griffin R. Forum on drug discovery, development, and translation. Washington, D.C.: Institute of Medicine; 2010.

[25] Fergusson D, Glass KC, Hutton B, Shapiro S. Randomized controlled trials of aprotinin in cardiac surgery: could clinical equipoise have stopped the bleeding? Clin Trials 2005;2:218−29.

[26] Berman JJ. Precancer: the beginning and the end of cancer. Sudbury: Jones and Bartlett; 2010.

[27] Mortality, total U.S. (1969−2005). Surveillance, Epidemiology, and End Results (SEER) Program <www.seer.cancer.gov>. National Cancer Institute, DCCPS, Surveillance Research Program, Cancer Statistics Branch, released April 2008. Underlying mortality data provided by NCHS <www.cdc.gov/nchs>.

[28] Berman JJ, Albores-Saavedra J, Bostwick D, Delellis R, Eble J, Hamilton SR, et al. Precancer: a conceptual working definition Results of a Consensus Conference. Cancer Detect Prev 2006;30(5):387−94.

[29] Berman JJ, Henson DE. The precancers: waiting for a classification. Human Pathol 2003;34:833−4.

[30] Ponten J. Precancer: biology, importance and possible prevention. Cold Spring Harbor, NY: Cold Spring Harbor Laboratory Press; 1998.

APPENDIX A

Index of Case Studies

APPENDIX *B*

Glossary

If triangles had a god, they would give him three sides.

Voltaire

Abandonware	Software that is abandoned (e.g., no longer updated, supported, distributed, or sold) after its economic value is depleted. Most of the software in existence today is abandonware.
Accuracy versus precision	Accuracy measures how close your data comes to being correct. Precision provides a measurement of reproducibility (i.e., whether repeated measurements of the same quantity produce the same result). Data can be accurate but imprecise. If you have a 10 pound object, and you report its weight as 7.2376 pounds, every time you weigh the object, then your precision is remarkable, but your accuracy is dismal.
Algorithm	A general computational method. In the past half century, many brilliant algorithms have been developed that can be applied to data repurposing studies [1,2].
Annotation	Annotation involves supplying data with additional data to provide further description, disambiguation (e.g., adding identifiers to distinguish the data from other data), links to other data, timestamps to mark when the data was created. One of the most important functions of annotation is to provide data elements with metadata that describes the data.
Child class	The direct or first generation subclass of a class. Sometimes referred to as the daughter class or, less precisely, as the subclass. See Glossary items, Parent class, Classification.

Class	A class is a group of objects that share a set of properties that define the class and that distinguish the members of the class from members of other classes. See Glossary item, Classification.
Classification	A system in which every object in a knowledge domain is assigned to a class within a hierarchy of classes. The properties of superclasses are inherited by the subclasses. Every class has one immediate superclass (i.e., the parent class), although a parent class may have more than one immediate subclass (child class). Objects do not change their class assignment in a classification, unless there was a mistake in the assignment. For example, a rabbit is always a rabbit, does not change into a tiger, and is not reassigned from Class Lagomorpha to Class Felidae. Classifications can be thought of as the simplest and most restrictive type of ontology and serve to reduce the complexity of a knowledge domain [3]. Classifications can be easily modeled in an object-oriented programming language and are nonchaotic (i.e., calculations performed on the members and classes of a classification should yield the same output, each time the calculation is performed). See Glossary items, Parent class, Child class.
Correlation distance	The correlation distance provides a measure of similarity between two variables. Two similar variables will rise and fall together, and it is this coordinated variation in value that is measured by correlation scores. See Glossary item, Pearson's correlation [4,5].
Curator	The word "curator" derives from the latin, "curatus," the same root for "curative," indicating that curators "take care of" things. A data curator collects data and ensures that there is an adequate protocol for verifying the data. In addition, the curator chooses appropriate nomenclatures for annotating the data, annotates the data, and

makes appropriate adjustments to data annotations when new versions of nomenclatures are made available or when one nomenclature is replaced by another.

Curse of dimensionality
As the number of attributes for data objects increases, the multidimensional attribute space becomes sparsely populated, and the distances between any two objects, even the two closest neighbors, become absurdly large. When you have thousands of dimensions (e.g., data values in a data record, cells in the rows of a spreadsheet), the space that holds the objects is so large that distances between objects become difficult or impossible to compute, and most computational algorithms become useless.

Dark data
Unstructured and ignored legacy data, presumed to account for most of the data in the "infoverse." The term takes its name from "dark matter" which is the invisible stuff that accounts for most of the gravitational attraction in the physical universe.

Data Quality Act
Passed as part of the FY 2001 Consolidated Appropriations Act (Pub. L. No. 106-554), the Act requires U.S. Federal Agencies to base their policies and regulations on high quality data and permits the public to challenge and correct inaccurate data [6]. Implicit in the Act is that data upon which public policy is decided must be shared with the public; otherwise the public would have no opportunity to challenge policies based on poor data and poor data analysis.

Data archeology
The process of recovering information held in abandoned or unpopular physical storage devices or in formats that are no longer widely recognized, and hence unsupported by most software applications. The definition encompasses truly ancient data, such as cuneiform inscriptions stored on clay tablets circa 3,300 BCE, and digital data stored on 5.25 inch floppy disks in Xyrite wordprocessor format, circa 1994.

Data cleaning	Synonymous with data fixing or data correcting, data cleaning is the process by which errors, inexplicable anomalies, and missing values are somehow handled. The options for data cleaning are three: correcting the error, deleting the error, or leaving it unchanged [7]. Data cleaning should not be confused with data scrubbing. See Glossary item, Data scrubbing.
Data fusion	Data fusion is very closely related to data integration. The subtle difference between the two concepts lies in the end result. Data fusion creates a new and accurate representation of the integrated data sources. Data integration is an on-the-fly usage of data pulled from different domains and, as such, does not produce a residual fused set of data.
Data integration	The process of drawing data from different sources and knowledge domains in a way that uses and preserves the identities of data objects and the relationships among the different data objects. The term "integration" should not be confused with a closely related term, "interoperability." An easy way to remember the difference is to note that integration applies to data; interoperability applies to software.
Data merging	A nonspecific term that would include data fusion, data integration, and any methods that facilitate the accrual of data derived from multiple sources. See Glossary items, Data fusion, Data Integration.
Data mining (alternate form, datamining)	The term "data mining" is closely related to "data repurposing" and both endeavors employ many of the same techniques. The same professionals who are involved in data mining efforts are likely to be involved in data repurposing efforts. In data mining, the data, and the expected purpose of the data, is "given" to the data miner. For example, using an adverse drug reaction database to determine if a drug produces an adverse reaction

would be a data mining project, not a data repurposing project.

Data munging | Refers to a multitude of tasks involved in preparing data for some intended purpose (e.g., data cleaning, data scrubbing, data transformation). Synonymous with data wrangling.

Data object | A set of metadata/data pairs assigned to a unique identifier. The idealized data object consists of a collection of zero or more data/metadata pairs (e.g., height—60 cm; weight—100 kg; name—John Smith), the name of the class of objects to which the object belongs (e.g., class Human), and a unique identifier string (e.g., 54823ksg93tjamv338ax95). Data objects in object-oriented programming languages are associated with specific sets of methods that operate exclusively on the object (i.e., so-called instance methods) or on all of the objects of the same class (i.e., class methods) or on objects of a common lineage (i.e., inherited methods). In practice, the most common data objects are simple data records, corresponding to a row in a spreadsheet or a line in a flat file.

Data versus datum | The singular form of data is datum, but the word "datum" has virtually disappeared from the computer science literature. The word "data" has assumed both singular and plural forms. In its singular form, it is a collective noun that refers to a single aggregation of many data points. Hence, current usage would be "The data is enormous," rather than "These data are enormous."

Data reduction | When a very large dataset is analyzed, it may be impractical or counterproductive to work with every element of the collected data. In such cases, the data analyst may choose to eliminate some of the data, or develop methods whereby the data is approximated. Some data scientists reserve the term "data reduction" for methods that reduce the dimensionality of multivariate datasets.

Data scraping	Pulling desired sections of a dataset or text, using software.
Data scrubbing	A term that is very similar to data deidentification and is sometimes used improperly as a synonym for data deidentification. Data scrubbing refers to the removal, from data records, of any information that is considered unwanted. This may include identifiers, private information, or any incriminating or otherwise objectionable language contained in data records, as well as any information deemed irrelevant to the purpose served by the record. See Glossary item, Deidentification.
Data sharing	Providing one's own data to another person or entity. This process may involve free or purchased data, and it may be done willingly, or under coercion, as in compliance with regulations, laws, or court orders.
Data wrangling	Jargon referring to a multitude of tasks involved in preparing data for eventual analysis. Synonymous with data munging [8].
Deep analytics	A jargon term glibly applied to advanced mathematical techniques used by modern data analysts. In a recent McKinsey report, the authors asserted that the US "faces a shortage of 140,000−190,000 people with deep analytical skills" [9].
Deidentification	The process of removing all of the links in a data record that can connect the information in the record to an individual. This usually includes the record identifier, demographic information (e.g., place of birth), personal information (e.g., birthdate), biometrics (e.g., fingerprints), and so on. The process of deidentification will vary based on the type of records included in the massive or complex data resource. See Glossary items, Reidentification, Data scrubbing.
Deidentification versus anonymization	Anonymization is a process whereby all the links between an individual and the individual's data record are irreversibly removed. The difference

between anonymization and deidentification is that anonymization is irreversible. Because anonymization is irreversible, the opportunities of verifying the quality of data are highly limited. For example, if someone suspects that samples have been switched in a dataset, thus putting the results of the study into doubt, an anonymized set of data would allow no opportunity to resolve the problem by returning to the original samples.

Dimensionality   The dimensionality of a data object consists of the number of attributes that describe the object. Depending on the design and content of the data structure that contains the data object (i.e., database, array, list of records, object instance, etc.), the attributes will be called by different names, including field, variable, parameter, feature, or property. Data objects with high dimensionality create computational challenges, and data analysts typically reduce the dimensionality of data objects wherever possible.

Encapsulation   The concept, from object-oriented programming, that a data object contains its associated data. The concept of encapsulation is tightly linked to the concept of introspection, the process of accessing the data encapsulated within a data object.

Epigrapher   A person who studies inscriptions. Usually refers to the study of ancient inscriptions, such as petroglyphs, Sumerian tablets, Swedish runestones, Mayan or Egyptian hieroglyphs. Epigraphers played an important role in deciphering the Mayan hieroglyphs. Epigraphers are included in the Glossary to emphasize that data repurposing employs a broad range of professionals, from many seemingly unrelated disciplines.

Euclidean distance   Two points $(x1, y1)$, $(x2, y2)$ in Cartesian coordinates are separated by a hypotenuse distance, that being the square root of the sum of the squares of the differences between the respective x-axis and *y*-axis coordinates. In *n*-dimensional space, the Euclidean distance between two points is the square root of the sum of the squares of the differences for each of the *n*-dimensional coordinates. Data objects are often characterized by multiple feature values, and these feature values can be listed as though they were coordinate values for an *n*-dimensional object. The smaller the Euclidean distance between two objects, the higher the similarity to each other. Several of the most popular correlation and clustering algorithms involve pairwise comparisons of the Euclidean distances between data objects in a data collection. Data scientists are not limited to scaled feature measurements such as length. For example, another type of distance measurement, the Mahalanobis distance, measures correlation differences among variables. Hence, the Mahalanobis distance is not influenced by the relative scale of the different feature attributes of objects. The Mahalanobis distance is commonly applied within clustering and classifier algorithms [10].

Fourier series
Periodic functions (i.e., functions with repeating trends in the data, including waveforms and periodic time series data) can be represented as the sum of oscillating functions (i.e., functions involving sines, cosines, or complex exponentials). The summation function is the Fourier series.

Grid
A collection of computers and computer resources that are coordinated to provide a desired functionality. The Grid is the intellectual predecessor of Cloud computing. Cloud computing is less physically and administratively restricted than Grid computing.

Heterogeneous data
Sets of data that are dissimilar with regard to content, purpose, format, organization, and annotations. One of the purposes of data science is to discover relationships among heterogeneous data sources. For example, epidemiologic datasets may be of service to molecular biologists who

hold gene sequence data on diverse human populations. The epidemiologic data is likely to contain different types of data values, annotated and formatted in a manner that is completely different from the data and annotations in a gene sequence database. The two types of related data, epidemiologic and genetic, have dissimilar content; hence they are heterogeneous to one another.

Identification The process of providing a data object with an identifier, or the process of distinguishing one data object from all other data objects on the basis of its associated identifier. See Glossary item, Identifier.

Identifier A string that is associated with a particular thing (e.g., person, document, transaction, data object), and not associated with any other thing [11]. Object identification usually involves permanently assigning a seemingly random sequence of numeric digits (0−9) and alphabet characters (a−z and A−Z) to a data object. The data object itself is not confined to being a data record. A data object can be an abstraction such as a class of objects or a number or a string or a variable. See Glossary item, Identification.

Immutability Immutability is the principle that data collected in a massive or complex data resource is permanent, and can never be modified. At first thought, it would seem that immutability is a ridiculous and impossible constraint. In the real world, mistakes are made, information changes, and the methods for describing information changes. This is all true, but the astute data manager knows how to accrue information into data objects without changing the pre-existing data. Methods for achieving this seemingly impossible trick are described in Section 6.5.

Indexes Every writer must search deeply into his or her soul to find the correct plural form of "index." Is it "indexes" or is it "indices"? Latinists insist that "indices" is the proper and exclusive plural form. Grammarians agree, reserving "indexes" for the third person singular verb form; "The student indexes his thesis." Nonetheless, popular usage of the plural of "index," referring to the section at the end of a book, is almost always "indexes," the form used herein.

Instance   An instance is a specific example of an object that is not itself a class or group of objects. For example, Tony the Tiger is an instance of the tiger species. Tony the Tiger is a unique animal and is not itself a group of animals or a class of animals. The terms instance, instance object, and object are sometimes used interchangeably, but the special value of the "instance" concept, in a system wherein everything is an object, is that it distinguishes members of classes (i.e., the instances), from the classes to which they belong.

Intellectual property   Data, software, algorithms, and applications that are created by an entity capable of ownership (e.g., humans, corporations, universities). The owner entity holds rights over the manner in which the intellectual property can be used and distributed. Protections for intellectual property may come in the form of copyrights, patents, and laws that apply to theft. Copyright applies to published information. Patents apply to novel processes and inventions. Certain types of intellectual property can only be protected by being secretive. For example, magic tricks cannot be copyrighted or patented; this is why magicians guard their intellectual property against theft. Intellectual property can be sold outright or used under a legal agreement (e.g., license, contract, transfer agreement, royalty, usage fee, and so on). Intellectual property can also be shared freely, while retaining ownership (e.g., open-source license, GNU license, FOSS license, Creative Commons license).

ISO (International Organization for Standardization)   A nongovernmental organization that develops international standards. See Glossary item, ISO 11179.

ISO 11179   The ISO standard for defining metadata, such as XML tags. The standard requires that the definitions for metadata used in XML (the so-called tags) be accessible and should include the following information for each tag: Name (the label assigned to the tag), Identifier (the unique identifier assigned to the tag), Version (the version of the tag), Registration Authority (the entity authorized to register the tag), Language (the language in which the tag is specified), Definition (a statement that clearly represents the concept and essential nature of the tag), Obligation (indicating whether the tag is required), Datatype (indicating the type of data that can be represented in the value of the tag), Maximum Occurrence (indicating any limit to the repeatability of the tag), and Comment (a remark describing how the tag might be used) [12]. See Glossary item, ISO.

K-means algorithm   The k-means algorithm assigns any number of data objects to one of k clusters [2]. The k-means algorithm should not be confused with the k-nearest neighbor algorithm.

K-nearest neighbor algorithm   A simple and popular classifier algorithm that assigns a class (in a pre-existing classification) to an object whose class is unknown [2]. The k-nearest neighbor is very simple. From a collection of data objects whose class is known, the algorithm computes the distances from the object of unknown class to the objects of known class. The most common class of the nearest k classed objects is assigned to the object of unknown class. The k-nearest neighbor algorithm, a classifier method, should not be confused with the k-means algorithm, a clustering method.

Legacy data   Data collected by an information system that has
                       been replaced by a newer system, and which
                       cannot be immediately integrated into the newer
                       system's database. For example, hospitals
                       regularly replace their hospital information
                       systems with new systems that promise greater
                       efficiencies, expanded services, or improved
                       interoperability with other information systems. In
                       many cases, the new system cannot readily
                       integrate the data collected from the older system.
                       The previously collected data becomes a legacy to
                       the new system. In many cases, legacy data is
                       simply "stored" for some arbitrary period. After a
                       decade or so, the hospital finds itself without any
                       staff members who are capable of locating,
                       understanding, or using the legacy data.
Linear regression   A method for obtaining a straight line through a
                       two-dimensional scatter plot. It is not, as it is
                       commonly believed, a "best fit" technique, but it
                       does minimize the sum of squared errors (in the y-
                       axis values) under the assumption that the x-axis
                       values are correct and exact. This means that you
                       would get a different straight line if you regress
                       x on y; rather than y on x. Linear regression is a
                       popular method that has been extended, modified,
                       and modeled for many different processes,
                       including machine learning. Data analysts who
                       use linear regression should be cautioned that it is
                       a method, much like the venerable P-value, that is
                       commonly misinterpreted [13]. See Glossary item,
                       P-value.
Machine learning   Refers to computer systems and software
                       applications that learn or improve as new data is
                       acquired. Examples would include language
                       translation software that improves in accuracy as
                       more and more language data is added to the
                       system; predictive software that improves as more
                       examples are obtained. Machine learning
                       applications include search engines, optical

character recognition software, speech recognition software, vision software, and neural networks. Machine learning systems are likely to use training datasets and test datasets. Machine learning usually involves making improvements on a well-defined task that can be assigned to a computer, and involves repurposing when the team that has been working on a project decides to apply the data to some other task.

Mean-field approximation
A method whereby the average behavior for a population of objects substitutes for the behavior of each and every object in the population. This method greatly simplifies calculations. It is based on the observation that large collections of objects can be characterized by their average behavior. Mean-field approximation has been used with great success to understand the behavior of gases, epidemics, crystals, viruses, and all manner of large population phenomena.

Meaning
In informatics, meaning is achieved when described data is bound to the unique identifier of a data object. "Jules J. Berman's height is 5 feet 11 inches," comes pretty close to being a meaningful statement. The statement contains data (5 feet 11 inches), and the data is described (height). The described data belongs to a unique object (Jules J. Berman). If this data were entered into a massive or complex data resource, it would need a unique identifier, to distinguish one instance of Jules J. Berman from all the other persons who are named Jules J. Berman. The statement would also benefit from a formal system that ensures that the metadata makes sense (e.g., What exactly is height, and does Jules J. Berman fall into a class of objects for which height is an allowable property?) and that the data is appropriate (e.g., Is 5 feet 11 inches an allowable measure of a person's height?). A statement with meaning does not need to be a true statement

(e.g., The height of Jules J. Berman was not 5 feet 11 inches when Jules J. Berman was an infant). See Glossary items, Semantics, Triple, RDF.

Meta-analysis   Combining data from multiple similar and comparable studies to produce a summary result. The hope is that by combining individual studies, the meta-analysis will carry greater credibility and accuracy than any single study. Three of the most recurring flaws in meta-analysis studies are selection bias (e.g., negative studies are often omitted from the literature), inadequate descriptions of the included sets of data (limitations on the length of articles yield incomplete methods sections), and nonrepresentative data (the published data is a small subset of the data collected by the original sets of researchers).

Metadata   The data that describes data. For example, a data point may consist of the number, "150." The metadata for the data may be the words "Weight, in pounds." A data point is useless without its metadata, and metadata is useless if it does not convey the information that adequately explains the data. In XML, the metadta/data annotation might be something like: <weight_in_pounds > 150 < /weight_in_pounds>. In the common spreadsheet, the data elements are the cells of the spreadsheet. The column headers are the metadata that describe the data values in the column, and the row headers are the record numbers that uniquely identify each record. See Glossary item, XML.

Missing values   Most complex datasets have missing data values. Somewhere along the line data elements were not entered, or records were lost, or some systemic error produced empty data fields. Large, complex datasets, collected from diverse sources, are almost certain to have missing data. Various mathematical approaches to missing data have been developed, commonly involving assigning values on a statistical basis, so-called imputation methods. The underlying assumption for such methods is that missing data arises at random. When missing data arises nonrandomly, there is no satisfactory statistical fix. The data curator must track down the source of the errors, and somehow rectify the situation. In either case, the issue of missing data introduces a potential bias, and it is crucial to fully document the method by which missing data is handled.

Modeling
Usually refers to the intellectual process of finding a mathematical expression (often, an equation) or a symbolic expression that describes or summarizes a system or a collection of data. For example, a formula may describe the distribution of the data and often predicts how the different variables will change with one another. One of the chief jobs of the data analyst is to derive simple rules to explain complex data.

Monte Carlo simulation
This technique was introduced in 1946 by John von Neumann, Stan Ulam, and Nick Metropolis [1]. For this technique, the computer generates random numbers and uses the resultant values to simulate repeated trials of a probabilistic event. Monte Carlo simulations can easily simulate various processes (e.g., Markov models and Poisson processes) and can be used to solve a wide range of problems [14,15]. The Achilles heel of the Monte Carlo simulation, when applied to enormous sets of data, is that so-called random number generators may introduce periodic (nonrandom) repeats over large stretches of data [16]. The wise analyst will avail himself of the best possible random number generators and will test his outputs for randomness. Various tests of randomness are available [17].

Multiclass inheritance
In ontologies, multiclass inheritance occurs when a child class has more than one parent class. For example, a member of Class House may have two different parent classes: Class Shelter and Class

Property. Multiclass inheritance is generally permitted in ontologies but is forbidden in one type of restrictive ontology known as a classification. See Glossary item, Classification, Parent class.

Multiple comparisons bias
When you compare a control group against a treated group using multiple hypotheses based on the effects of many different measured parameters, you will eventually encounter statistical significance, based on chance alone. For example, if you are trying to determine whether a population that has been treated with a particular drug is likely to suffer a serious clinical symptom, and you start looking for statistically significant associations (e.g., liver disease, kidney disease, prostate disease, heart disease, etc.), then eventually you will find an organ in which disease is more likely to occur in the treated group than in the untreated group.

Namespace
A namespace is the metadata realm in which a metadata tag applies. The purpose of a namespace is to distinguish metadata tags that have the same name, but a different meaning. For example, within a single XML file, the metadata term "date" may be used to signify a calendar date, or the fruit, or the social engagement. To avoid confusion, the metadata term is given a prefix that is associated with a Web document that defines the term within the document's namespace.

Negative study bias
When a project produces negative results (fails to confirm a hypothesis), there may be little enthusiasm to publish the work [18]. When statisticians analyze the results from many different published manuscripts (i.e., perform a meta-analysis), their work is biased by the pervasive absence of negative studies [19]. In the field of medicine, negative study bias creates a false sense that every kind of treatment yields positive results.

Neural network   A dynamic system in which outputs are calculated by a summation of weighted functions operating on inputs. The weights for the individual functions are determined by a learning process, simulating the learning process hypothesized for human neurons. In the computer model, individual functions that contribute to a correct output (based on the training data) have their weights increased (strengthening their influence to the calculated output). Over the past 10 or 15 years, neural networks have lost some favor in the artificial intelligence community. They can become computationally complex for very large sets of multidimensional input data. More importantly, the results produced by complex neural networks cannot be understood or explained by humans, endowing these systems with a "magical" quality that some scientists find unacceptable. See Glossary items, nongeneralizable predictor, Overfitting.

New data   It is natural to think of certain objects as being "new," meaning, with no prior existence; and other objects being "old," having persisted from an earlier time. In truth, there are very few "new" objects in our universe. Most objects arise in a continuum, through a transformation or a modification of an old object. For example, embryos are simply cellular growths that develop from pre-existing gonocytes, and the development of an embryo into a newborn organism follows ancient instructions written by combined fragments of pre-existing DNA sequences. When we speak of "new" data, alternately known as prospectively acquired data or as prospective data, we must think in terms that relate the new data to the "old" data that preceded it. For example the air temperature 1 min from now is largely determined by weather events that are occurring now, and the weather occurring now is largely determined by all of the weather events that have occurred in the history of our planet. Data scientists have a pithy aphorism that captures the entangled relationship between "new" and "old" data: "Every prospective study becomes a retrospective study on day 2."

Nomenclature mapping
Specialized nomenclatures employ specific names for concepts that are included in other nomenclatures, under other names. For example, various US regions have their terminology for a large, multilayered sandwich built into a round roll, and known variously as sub (i.e., submarine sandwich), hoagie, grinder, and hero. In Louisiana, such sandwiches are known a "po' boys," a term that might not be generally understood in New Hampshire. Likewise, medical specialists often preserve their favored names for concepts that cross into different fields of medicine. For example, the term that pathologists use for a certain begin fibrous tumor of the skin is "fibrous histiocytoma," a term for which dermatologists use "dermatofibroma." The names applied to the physiologic responses caused by a reversible cerebral vasoconstrictive event may include thunderclap headache, Call-Fleming syndrome, benign angiopathy of the central nervous system, postpartum angiopathy, migrainous vasospasm, and migraine angiitis. The choice of term will vary depending on the medical specialty of the treating physician (e.g., neurologist, rheumatologist, obstetrician). To mitigate the discord among nomenclatures, lexicographers may undertake a harmonization project, in which nomenclatures with equivalent concepts are mapped to one another.

Nongeneralizable predictor
Sometimes Big Data analysis can yield results that are true, but nongeneralizable (i.e., irrelevant to everything outside the set of data objects under study). The most useful scientific findings are generalizable (e.g., the laws of physics operate on the planet Jupiter or the

star Alpha Centauri much as they do on earth). Many popular analytic methods are not generalizable because they produce predictions that only apply to highly restricted sets of data; or the predictions are not explainable by any underlying theory that relates input data with the calculated predictions.

Nonparametric statistics   Statistical methods that are not based on the parameters (e.g., mean, standard deviation, normal distribution) employed in the familiar methods of descriptive statistics (i.e., in parametric statistics). In practical terms, nonparametric statistics are used when a normal population distribution cannot be assumed.

Notation 3   Also called n3. A syntax for expressing assertions as triples (unique subject + metadata + data). Notation 3 expresses the same information as the more formal RDF syntax, but n3 is compact and easy for humans to read [20]. Both n3 and RDF can be parsed and equivalently tokenized (i.e., broken into elements that can be reorganized in a different format, such as a database record). See Glossary item, RDF.

Object-oriented programming   In object-oriented programming, all data objects must belong to one of the classes built into the language or to a class created by the programmer. Class methods are subroutines that belong to a class. The members of a class have access to the class methods. There is a hierarchy of classes (with superclasses and subclasses). A data object can access any method from any superclass of its class. All object-oriented programming languages operate under this general strategy. The most important differences among the various object-oriented programming languages relate to syntax (i.e., the required style in which data objects call their available methods) and content (the language-specific built-in classes and methods available to objects). See Glossary item, Data object.

One-way hash   A one-way hash is an algorithm that transforms one string into another string (a fixed length sequence of seemingly random characters) in such a way that the original string cannot be calculated by operations on the one-way hash value (i.e., the calculation is one-way only). One-way hash values can be calculated for any string, including a person's name, a document, or an image. For any input string, the resultant one-way hash will always be the same. If a single byte of the input string is modified, the resulting one-way hash will be changed, and will have a totally different sequence than the one-way hash sequence calculated for the unmodified string. The one-way hash values can be made sufficiently long (e.g., 256 bits) that a hash string collision (i.e., the occurrence of two different input strings with the same one-way hash output value) is negligible. Clever variations on one-way hash algorithms have been repurposed as identifier systems [21−24].

Ontology   An ontology is a collection of classes and their relationships to one another. Ontologies are usually rule-based systems (i.e., membership in a class is determined by one or more class rules). Two properties, when applied, distinguish ontologies from classifications. Ontologies permit classes to have more than one parent class and more than one child class. For example, the class of automobiles may be a direct subclass of "motorized devices" and a direct subclass of "mechanized transporters." In addition, an instance of a class can be an instance of any number of additional classes. For example, a Lamborghini may be a member of class "automobiles" and class "luxury items." This means that the lineage of an instance in an ontology can be highly complex, with a single instance occurring in multiple classes. Because recursive relations are permitted, it is possible to build an ontology wherein a class is both an ancestor class and a descendant class, of itself! A classification is a highly restrained ontology wherein instances can belong to only one class, and each class may have only one direct parent class. Because classifications have an enforced linear hierarchy, they can be easily modeled, and the lineage of any instance can be traced unambiguously. See Glossary item, Classification.

Open access   A document is open access if its complete contents are available to the public. Open access applies to documents in the same manner as open source applies to software.

Open source   Software is open source if the source code is available to anyone who has access to the software.

Outlier   Outliers are extreme data values (i.e. values that lie beyond anything you would expect to see). The occurrence of outliers hinders the task of developing models, equations, or curves that closely fit all the available data. In some cases, outliers are simply mistakes that can be ignored by the data analyst. In other cases, the outlier may be the most important data in the dataset. Every data analyst must develop a reasonable approach to dealing with outliers, based on the kinds of data under study.

Overfitting   Overfitting occurs when a formula describes a set of data very closely, but does not lead to any sensible explanation for the behavior of the data, and does not predict the behavior of comparable datasets. In the case of overfitting, the formula is said to describe the noise of the system, rather than the characteristic behavior of the system. Overfitting occurs frequently with models that perform iterative approximations on training data, coming closer and closer to the training dataset with each iteration. Neural networks are an example of a data modeling strategy that is prone to overfitting [10].

P-value   The *P*-value is the probability of getting a set of
                   results that are as extreme or more extreme than
                   the set of results you observed, assuming that
                   the null hypothesis is true (that there is no
                   statistical difference between the results). The
                   P-value has come under great criticism over the
                   decades, with a growing consensus that the
                   P-value is often misinterpreted, used incorrectly,
                   or used in situations wherein it does not apply
                   [25]. Repeated samplings of data from large
                   datasets will produce small *P*-values that cannot
                   be usefully related to statistical significance. It is
                   best to think of the *P*-value as just another piece
                   of information that tells you something about
                   how sets of observations compare with one
                   another; and not as a test of statistical
                   significance.

Parent class   The class that is the next higher class (i.e., the
                   direct superclass) to the child class it contains.
                   For example, in the classification of living
                   organisms, Class Vertebrata is the parent class
                   of Class Gnathostomata. Class Gnathostomata
                   is the parent class of Class Teleostomi. In a
                   classification, which imposes single class
                   inheritance, each child class has exactly one
                   parent class; whereas one parent class may have
                   several different child classes. Furthermore,
                   some classes, in particular the bottom class in the
                   lineage, have no child classes (i.e., a class need not
                   always be a superclass of other classes). For this
                   reason, a class can be fully defined by its
                   properties, its membership (i.e., the instances that
                   belong to the class), and by the name of its parent
                   class. When we list all of the classes in a
                   classification, in any order, we can always
                   reconstruct the complete class lineage, in their
                   correct lineage and branchings, if we know the
                   name of each class's parent class. See Glossary
                   items, Instance, Child class, Superclass.

Parthenogenesis   The development of an organism from an unfertilized egg. Parthenogenesis occurs in many plants and in some animal species.

Pearson's correlation   All similarity scores are based on comparing one data object with another, attribute by attribute, usually summing the squares of the differences in magnitude for each attribute, and using the calculation to compute a final outcome, known as the correlation score. One of the most popular correlation methods is Pearson's correlation, which produces a score that can vary from -1 to $+1$. Two objects with a high score (near $+1$) are highly similar. Pearson's correlation can be used to compare complex data objects that differ in size and content. For example, Pearson's correlation can compare two different books, using the terms contained in each book and the number of occurrences of each term [26].

Plesionymy   Nearly synonymous words or pairs of words that are sometimes synonymous; other times not. For example, the noun forms of "smell" and "odor" are synonymous. As verb forms, "smell" applies, but odor does not. You can small a fish, but you cannot odor a fish. Smell and odor are plesionyms. Plesionymy is another challenge for machine translators.

Predictive analytics   This term most often applies to a collection of techniques that have been used, with great success, in marketing. These are: recommenders, classifiers, and clustering [27]. Though all of these techniques can be used for purposes other than marketing, they are often described in marketing terms: recommenders (e.g., predicting which products a person might prefer to buy), profile clustering (e.g., grouping individuals into marketing clusters based on the similarity of their profiles), and product classifiers (e.g., assigning a product or individual to a prediction category, based on a set of features). See Glossary item, Recommender.

Primary data   The original set of data collected to serve a particular purpose or to answer a particular set of questions, and intended for use by the same individuals who collected the data.

Principal component analysis   A computationally intensive method for reducing the dimensionality of datasets [13]. This method takes a list of parameters and reduces it to a smaller list of variables, with each component of the smaller list constructed from combinations of variables in the longer list. Principal component analysis indicates which variables in both the original and the new list are least correlated with the other variables.

Privacy versus confidentiality   The concepts of confidentiality and of privacy are often confused, and it is useful to clarify their separate meanings. Confidentiality is the process of keeping a secret with which you have been entrusted. You break confidentiality if you reveal the secret to another person. You violate privacy when you use the secret to annoy the person whose confidential information was acquired. If you give me your unlisted telephone number in confidence, then I am expected to protect this confidentiality by never revealing the number to other persons. I may also be expected to protect your privacy by never using the telephone number to call you at all hours of the day and night. In this case, the same information object (unlisted telephone number) is encumbered by confidentiality and privacy obligations.

Protocol   A set of instructions, policies, or fully described procedures for accomplishing a service, operation, or task. Data is generated and collected according to protocols. There are protocols for conducting experiments, and there are protocols for measuring the results. There are protocols for choosing the human subjects included in a clinical trial, and there are protocols for interacting with the human subjects during the course of the trial. All network communications are conducted via protocols; the Internet operates under a protocol (TCP-IP, Transmission Control Protocol-Internet Protocol).

Public domain Data that is not owned by an entity. Public domain materials include documents whose copyright terms have expired, materials produced by the federal government, materials that contain no creative content (i.e., materials that cannot be copyrighted), or materials donated to the public domain by the entity that held copyright. Public domain data can be accessed, copied, and redistributed without violating piracy laws. It is important to note that plagiarism laws and rules of ethics apply to public domain data. You must properly attribute authorship to public domain documents. If you fail to attribute authorship or if you purposefully and falsely attribute authorship to the wrong person (e.g., yourself), then this would be an unethical act and an act of plagiarism.

Query One of the first sticking points in any discussion of heterogeneous database queries is the definition of "query." Informaticians use the term "query" to mean a request for records that match a specific set of data element features (e.g., name, age, etc.). Ontologists think of a query as a question that matches the competence of the ontology (i.e., a question for which the ontology can infer an answer).

RDF (Resource Description Framework) A syntax expressed in XML notation that formally expresses assertions in three components, the so-called RDF triple. The RDF triple consists of a uniquely identified subject plus a metadata descriptor for the data plus a data element. Triples are necessary and sufficient to create statements that convey meaning. Triples can be aggregated with other triples from the same dataset or from other datasets, so long as each triple pertains to a unique subject that is identified equivalently through the datasets. Enormous datasets of RDF triples can be merged or functionally integrated with other massive or complex data resources. See Glossary items, Notation 3, Semantics, Triple, XML.

RDF Schema   A document containing a list of classes, their definitions, and the names of the parent class(es) for each class. In an RDF Schema, the list of classes is followed by a list of properties that apply to one or more classes in the Schema. After an RDF Schema is prepared, it is typically posted onto the Internet, as a public Web page, with a unique Web address. Anyone can incorporate the classes and properties of the RDF Schema into their own RDF documents by linking to the web address of the RDF Schema.

Reflection   A programming technique wherein a computer program will modify itself, at run time, based on information it acquires through introspection (see Section 2.5). For example, a computer program may iterate over a collection of data objects, examining the self-descriptive information for each object in the collection (i.e., object introspection). If the information indicates that the data object belongs to a particular class of objects, the program might call a method appropriate for the class. The program executes in a manner determined by descriptive information obtained during run time; metaphorically reflecting upon the purpose of its computational task.

Reanalysis   Producing a new analysis of the same set of data, beginning with the same question.

Recommender   A collection of methods for predicting the preferences of individuals. Recommender methods often rely on one or two simple assumptions: (i) if an individual expresses a preference for a certain type of product, and the individual encounters a new product that is similar to a previously preferred product, then he is likely to prefer the new product; (ii) if an individual expresses preferences that are similar to the preferences expressed by a cluster of individuals, and if the members of the cluster prefer a product that the individual has not yet encountered, then the individual will most likely prefer the product. See Glossary items, Predictive analytics, Classifier.

Reidentification   A term casually applied to any instance whereby information can be linked to a specific person, after the links between the information and the person associated with the information were removed. Used this way, the term reidentification connotes an insufficient deidentification process. In the healthcare industry, the term "reidentification" means something else entirely. In the United States, regulations define "reidentification" under the "Standards for Privacy of Individually Identifiable Health Information" [28]. Reidentification is defined therein as a legally valid process whereby deidentified records can be linked back to their human subjects, under circumstances deemed compelling by a privacy board. Reidentification is typically accomplished via a confidential list of links between human subject names and deidentified records, held by a trusted party. As used by the healthcare industry, reidentification only applies to the approved process of re-establishing the identity of a deidentified record. When a human subject is identified through fraud, trickery, or through the deliberate use of computational methods to break the confidentiality of insufficiently deidentified records, the term "reidentification" would not apply [10].

Representation bias   Occurs when the population sampled does not represent the population intended for study. For example, the population for which the normal range of prostate specific antigen (PSA) was based, was selected from a county in the state of Minnesota. The male population under study consisted almost exclusively of white men (i.e., virtually no African-Americans, Asians, Hispanics, etc.). It may have been assumed that PSA levels would not vary with race. It was eventually determined that the normal PSA ranges varied greatly by race [29]. The Minnesota data, though plentiful, did not represent racial subpopulations.

Reproducibility   Reproducibility is achieved when repeated studies produce the same results over and over. Reproducibility is closely related to validation, which is achieved when you draw the same conclusions, from the data, over and over again. Implicit in the concept of "reproducibility" is that the original research must somehow convey the means by which the study can be reproduced. This usually requires the careful recording of methods, algorithms, and materials. In some cases, reproducibility requires access to the data produced in the original studies. If there is no feasible way for scientists to undertake a reconstruction of the original study, or if the results obtained in the original study cannot be obtained in subsequent attempts, then the work is considered irreproducible. See Glossary items, Validation, Verification.

Semantics   The study of meaning. In the context of data science, semantics is the technique of creating meaningful assertions about data objects. A meaningful assertion, as used here, is a triple consisting of an identified data object, a data value, and a descriptor for the data value. In practical terms, semantics involves making assertions about data objects (i.e., making triples), combining assertions about data objects (i.e., merging triples), and assigning data objects to classes; hence relating triples to other triples. As a word of warning, few informaticians would define semantics in these terms, but most definitions for semantics are functionally equivalent to the definition offered here. See Glossary items, Triple, RDF.

Similarity versus Relationship

The distinction between relationships among objects and similarities among objects is one of the most fundamental concepts in data analysis; yet it is commonly misunderstood. Relationships are the fundamental properties of an object that account for its behavior and its interactions with other objects. Mathematical equations establish relationships among the variables of the equation. For example, mass is related to force by its velocity. An object is a member of a particular class if it has a relationship to all of the other members of the class (e.g., all rodents have gnawing teeth; all eukaryotic organisms have a nucleus). Related objects tend to be similar to one another, but these similarities occur as the consequence of their relationships; not vice versa. For example, you may have many similarities to your father; but, you are similar to your father because you are related to him. You are not related to him because you are similar to him. Here is a specific example that demonstrates the difference between a similarity and a relationship. You look up at the clouds, and you see the shape of a lion. The cloud has a tail, like a lion's tale, and a fluffy head, like a lion's mane. With a little imagination, the mouth of the lion seems to roar down from the sky. You have succeeded in finding similarities between the cloud and a lion. If you look at a cloud and you imagine a tea kettle producing a head of steam, and you recognize that the physical forces that create a cloud and the physical forces that produce steam from a heated kettle are the same, then you have found a relationship. Relationships help us describe how objects interact with one another. Without science-based relationships, reality makes no sense.

String
A string is a sequence of characters (i.e., letters, numbers, punctuation). This book is a long string. The complete sequence of the human genome (3 billion characters, with each character an A, T, G, or C) is an even longer string. Every subsequence of a string is also a string.

Subclass
A class in which every member belongs to some higher class (i.e., a superclass) within the class hierarchy. Members of a subclass have properties specific to the subclass, and can access all of the methods specific to the subclass. Because every member of a subclass is also a member of the superclass, the members of a subclass have the defining properties of the superclass and have access to methods of the superclass. For example, all mammals have mammary glands because mammary glands are a defining property of the mammal class. In addition, all mammals have vertebrae because the class of mammals is a subclass of the class of vertebrates. See Glossary item, Child class.

Superclass
A class that contains subclasses. For example, in the classification of living organisms, the class of vertebrates is a superclass of the class of mammals. See Glossary items, Subclass, Parent class.

Support vector machine (SVM)
A machine learning technique that classifies objects. The method starts with a training set consisting of two classes of objects as input. The support vector machine computes a hyperplane, in a multidimensional space, that separates objects of the two classes. The dimension of the hyperspace is determined by the number of dimensions or attributes associated with the objects. Additional objects (i.e., test set objects) are assigned membership in one class or the other, depending on which side of the hyperplane they reside.

Syntax
Syntax is the standard form or structure of a statement. What we know as English grammar is

equivalent to the syntax for the English language. Charles Mead distinctly summarized the difference between syntax and semantics: "Syntax is structure; semantics is meaning" [30].

Taxonomy

The definition varies, but as used here, a taxonomy is the collection of named instances (class members) in a classification. When you see a schematic showing class relationships, with individual classes represented by geometric shapes and the relationships represented by arrows or connecting lines between the classes, then you are essentially looking at the structure of a classification. You can think of building a taxonomy as the act of pouring all of the names of all of the instances into their proper classes within the classification schematic. A taxonomy is similar to a nomenclature; the difference is that in a taxonomy, every named instance must have an assigned class.

Term extraction algorithms

Terms are phrases, most often noun phrases, and sometimes individual words, that have a precise meaning within a knowledge domain. For example, "software validation," "RDF triple," and "WorldWide Telescope" are examples of terms that might appear in the index or the glossary of this book. The most useful terms might appear up to a dozen times in the text, but when they occur on every page, their value as a searchable item is diminished; there are just too many instances of the term to be of practical value. Hence, terms are sometimes described as noun phrases that have low-frequency and high information content. Various algorithms are available to extract candidate terms from textual documents. The candidate terms can be examined by a curator who determines whether they should be included in the index created for the document from which they were extracted. The curator may also compare the extracted candidate terms against a standard nomenclature, to determine

	whether the candidate terms should be added to the nomenclature [10].
Thesaurus	A vocabulary that groups together synonymous terms. A thesaurus is very similar to a nomenclature. There are two minor differences. Nomenclatures do not always group terms by synonymy; and nomenclatures are often restricted to a well-defined topic or knowledge domain (e.g., names of stars, infectious diseases, etc.).
Timestamp	Many data objects are temporal events and all temporal events must be given a timestamp indicating the time that the event occurred, using a standard measurement for time. The timestamp must be accurate, persistent, and immutable. The Unix epoch time (equivalent to the Posix epoch time) is available for most operating systems and consists of the number of seconds that have elapsed since January 1, 1970, midnight, Greenwich mean time. The Unix epoch time can easily be converted into any other standard representation of time. The duration of any event can be easily calculated by subtracting the beginning time from the ending time. Because the timing of events can be maliciously altered, scrupulous data managers employ a trusted timestamp protocol by which a timestamp can be verified. A trusted timestamp must be accurate, persistent, and immutable.
Transform	A transform is a mathematical operation that takes a function or a time series (e.g., values obtained at intervals of time) and transforms it into something else. An inverse transform takes the transform function and produces the original function. Transforms are useful when there are operations that can be more easily performed on the transformed function than on the original function. One of the most versatile and powerful transforms is the Fast Fourier transform, which can be computed with great speed on modern computers.

Triple	In computer semantics, a triple is an identified data object associated with a data element and the description of the data element. In theory, all datasets can be designed as collections of triples. See Glossary items, Introspection, Data object, Semantics, RDF.
Uniqueness	For data scientists, uniqueness is achieved when a data object is associated with a unique identifier (i.e., a character string that has not been assigned to any other object).
Universally Unique Identifier	See Glossary item, UUID.
UUID	UUID (Universally Unique IDentifier) is a protocol for assigning identifiers to data objects, without using a central registry. UUIDs were originally used in the Apollo Network Computing System [31].
Validation	Validation is the process that checks whether the data can be applied in a manner that fulfills its intended purpose. This often involves showing that correct conclusions can be obtained from a competent analysis of the data [32]. See Glossary items, Verification, Reproducibility.
Variable	In algebra, a variable is a quantity, in an equation, that can change; as opposed to a constant, that cannot change. In computer science, a variable can be perceived as a container that can be assigned a value. If you assign the integer 7 to a container named "x", then "x" equals 7, until you reassign some other value to the container (i.e., variables are mutable). In most computer languages, when you issue a command assigning a value to a new (undeclared) variable, the variable automatically comes into existence to accept the assignment. The process whereby an object comes into existence, because its existence was implied by an action (such as value assignment), is called reification.
Verification	The process by which data is checked to determine that it was obtained properly

	(i.e., according to approved protocols), and that the data measures what it was intended to measure, on the correct specimens. Verification is different from validation. Verification is performed on data, whereas validation is done on the results of data analysis. See Glossary item, Validation.
Vocabulary	A comprehensive collection of the words used in a knowledge domain. The term "vocabulary" and the term "nomenclature" are nearly synonymous. In common usage, a vocabulary is a list of words and typically includes a wide range of terms and classes of terms. Nomenclatures typically focus on a class of terms within a vocabulary (e.g., a nomenclature might be devoted to the names of astronomical bodies).
XML (eXtensible Markup Language)	a syntax for marking data values with descriptors (metadata). The descriptors are commonly known as tags. In XML, every data value is enclosed by a start tag, indicating that a value will follow, and an end tag, indicating that a value preceded the tag. For example: <name> Jules Berman </name>. The enclosing angle brackets, " < >," and the end-tag marker, "/," are hallmarks of XML markup. This simple but powerful relationship between metadata and data allows us to employ metadata/data pairs as though they were miniature databases. The semantic value of XML becomes apparent when we bind a metadata/data pair with a unique object, forming a so-called triple. See Glossary items, Triple, Meaning, Semantics.

REFERENCES

[1] Cipra BA. The best of the 20th century: editors name top 10 algorithms. SIAM News May 2000;33(4).

[2] Wu X, Kumar V, Quinlan JR, Ghosh J, Yang Q, Motoda H, et al. Top 10 algorithms in data mining. Knowl Inf Syst 2008;14:1–37.

[3] Patil N, Berno AJ, Hinds DA, Barrett WA, Doshi JM, Hacker CR, et al. Blocks of limited haplotype diversity revealed by high-resolution scanning of human chromosome 21. Science 2001;294:1719–23.

[4] Reshef DN, Reshef YA, Finucane HK, Grossman SR, McVean G, Turnbaugh PJ, et al. Detecting novel associations in large data sets. Science 2011;334:1518–24.

[5] Szekely GJ, Rizzo ML. Brownian distance covariance. Ann Appl Stat 2009;3:1236–65.

[6] Guidelines for ensuring and maximizing the quality, objectivity, utility, and integrity of information disseminated by federal agencies. Fed Regist 2002;67(36).

[7] Van den Broeck J, Cunningham SA, Eeckels R, Herbst K. Data cleaning: detecting, diagnosing, and editing data abnormalities. PLoS Med 2005;2:e267.

[8] Lohr S. For big-data scientists, "janitor work" is key hurdle to insights. The New York Times; August 17, 2014.

[9] Manyika J, Chui M, Brown B, Bughin J, Dobbs R, Roxburgh C, et al. Big data: The next frontier for innovation, competition, and productivity. McKinsey Global Institute; June, 2011.

[10] Berman JJ. Principles of big data: preparing, sharing, and analyzing complex information. Burlington, MA: Morgan Kaufmann; 2013.

[11] Paskin N. Identifier interoperability: a report on two recent ISO activities. D-Lib Magazine 2006;12:1–23.

[12] ISO/IEC 11179, Information Technology—Metadata registries. ISO/IEC JTC1 SC32 WG2 Development/Maintenance. Available from: <http://metadata-standards.org/11179/> [accessed 02.11.14].

[13] Janert PK. Data analysis with open source tools. Sebastopol, CA: O'Reilly Media; 2010.

[14] Berman JJ, Moore GW. The role of cell death in the growth of preneoplastic lesions: a Monte Carlo simulation model. Cell Prolif 1992;25:549–57.

[15] Berman JJ, Moore GW. Spontaneous regression of residual tumor burden: prediction by Monte Carlo Simulation. Anal Cellul Pathol 1992;4:359–68.

[16] Sainani K. Error: what biomedical computing can learn from its mistakes. Biomed Comput Rev 2011;12–19.

[17] Marsaglia G, Tsang WW. Some difficult-to-pass tests of randomness. J Stat Softw 2002;7:1–8. Available from: <http://www.jstatsoft.org/v07/i03/paper> [accessed 25.09.12].

[18] McGauran N, Wieseler B, Kreis J, Schuler Y, Kolsch H, Kaiser T. Trials 2010;11:37. Available from: <http://www.trialsjournal.com/content/11/1/37> [accessed 01.01.15].

[19] Dickersin K, Rennie D. Registering clinical trials. JAMA 2003;290:51.

[20] Berman JJ, Moore GW. Implementing an RDF Schema for Pathology Images 2007. Available from: <http://www.julesberman.info/spec2img.htm> [accessed 01.01.15].

[21] Faldum A, Pommerening K. An optimal code for patient identifiers. Comput Methods Programs Biomed 2005;79:81–8.

[22] Rivest R. Request for comments: 1321, the MD5 message-digest algorithm. Network Working Group. <https://www.ietf.org/rfc/rfc1321.txt> [accessed 01.01.15].

[23] Bouzelat H, Quantin C, Dusserre L. Extraction and anonymity protocol of medical file. Proc AMIA Annu Fall Symp 1996;1996:323–7.

[24] Quantin CH, Bouzelat FA, Allaert AM, Benhamiche J, Faivre J, Dusserre L. Automatic record hash coding and linkage for epidemiological followup data confidentiality. Methods Inf Med 1998;37:271–7.

[25] Cohen J. The earth is round ($p < .05$). Am Psychol 1994;49:997–1003.

[26] Berman JJ. Methods in medical informatics: fundamentals of healthcare programming in perl, python, and ruby. Boca Raton, FL: Chapman and Hall; 2010.

[27] Owen S, Anil R, Dunning T, Friedman E. Mahout in action. Shelter Island, NY: Manning Publications Co.; 2012.

[28] Department of Health and Human Services. 45 CFR (Code of Federal Regulations), Parts 160 through 164. Standards for privacy of individually identifiable health information (Final Rule). Fed Regist December 28, 2000;65(250):82461−510.

[29] Sawyer R, Berman JJ, Borkowski A, Moore GW. Elevated prostate-specific antigen levels in black men and white men. Mod Pathol 1996;9:1029−32.

[30] Mead CN. Data interchange standards in healthcare IT—computable semantic interoperability: now possible but still difficult, do we really need a better mousetrap? J Healthcare Inf Manag 2006;20:71−8.

[31] Leach P, Mealling M, Salz R. A universally unique identifier (UUID) URN namespace. Network Working Group, Request for Comment 4122, Standards Track. Available from: <http://www.ietf.org/rfc/rfc4122.txt> [accessed 01.01.15].

[32] Committee on Mathematical Foundations of Verification, Validation, and Uncertainty Quantification, Board on Mathematical Sciences and Their Applications, Division on Engineering and Physical Sciences, National Research Council. Assessing the reliability of complex models: mathematical and statistical foundations of verification, validation, and uncertainty quantification. National Academy Press; 2012. Available from: <http://www. nap.edu/catalog.php?record_id=13395> [accessed 01.01.15].

Printed in the United States
By Bookmasters